Perhaps you've heard the old saying,
"*Behind* every good man stands a good woman."
If we were to revise that saying for today, I believe it might go,
"*Beside* every good man stands a good woman."

Through my experiences and the lives of other women, I've examined dozens of issues that affect women at the core of our identities: our childhoods, our parents, our dreams, our failures, our longings, our disappointments. Out of these various threads of our life's fabric, one bold pattern emerges in every woman's life. Put simply: the men in our lives.

Certainly what we need from and give to our men varies with the seasons of our lives and the roles we play. Yet all of these interactions affect who we are and how we see ourselves. This is the territory I'd like to explore together in these pages.

—from BESIDE EVERY GOOD MAN

"There are numerous valuable lessons in BESIDE EVERY GOOD MAN."   —*QBR The Black Book Review*

"Ms. Jakes imparts a great deal of wisdom throughout the pages of her book . . . Her tone is gentle . . . I'd recommend BESIDE EVERY GOOD MAN to all women whose strength sometimes falters."   —MyShelf.com

"Jakes offers a new spin on the age-old question: Can men and women get along? She does so with style, class, and an excellent storytelling manner. Even women who aren't in relationships may find this book helpful for the future, or even for their present."   —Shades of Woman.com

$\mathscr{B}$ESIDE EVERY GOOD MAN

---

*Loving Myself
While Standing by Him*

Serita Ann Jakes

WARNER
Faith®

NEW YORK BOSTON NASHVILLE

Unless otherwise noted, Scripture references are taken from
THE NEW KING JAMES VERSION. Copyright © 1979, 1980, 1982,
Thomas Nelson, Inc., Publishers.
Scriptures noted NIV are taken from the HOLY BIBLE:
NEW INTERNATIONAL VERSION ®. Copyright © 1973, 1978, 1984 by
International Bible Society. Used by permission of Zondervan
Publishing House. All rights reserved.
Scriptures noted NASB are taken from the New American Standard
Bible®, Copyright © 1960, 1962, 1963, 1968, 1972, 1975, 1977, 1995
by The Lockman Foundation. Used by permission.
Scriptures noted CEV are taken from THE CONTEMPORARY
VERSION. © 1991 by the American Bible Society. Used by permission.

Warner Faith

Time Warner Book Group
1271 Avenue of the Americas, New York, NY 10020
Visit our Web site at www.twbookmark.com.

Warner Faith® and the Warner Faith logo are trademarks of
Time Warner Book Group Inc.

Printed in the United States of America
Originally published in hardcover by Warner Books.
First Warner Books Trade Printing: November 2004
10 9 8 7 6 5 4 3 2 1

The Library of Congress has cataloged the hardcover edition as follows:
Jakes, Serita Ann.
     Beside every good man : loving myself while standing by him /
Serita Ann Jakes.—1st Warner Books ed.
     p. cm.
     ISBN 0-446-53130-8
     1. Christian women—Religious life. 2. Women—Conduct of life.
I. Title.
     BV4527.J32 2003
     248.8'43—dc22   2003015156
ISBN: 0-446-69340-5 (pbk.)

Cover Design by Julia Kushnivsky
Photo by Birgit Utech/Photonica

To My Husband, who holds my heart and holds my hand as
we walk the steps ordered by God.

To My Baby Boys, as I stand in the wings and watch them
toddle into their destiny.

To My Big Brothers and My Little Brother, who stepped in
and guarded the little girl in me.

To My Daddy and My Poppa, who left footprints on my
heart as they took their journey beyond heaven's gate.

Special thanks

To Dudley Delff, with whom I shared my memoirs and my
dreams and whose hand became the pen of a ready writer.

To Warner Books, for encouraging me out of my silence.

To Cammy, My Girl Friday, who keeps me from day to day
on task and moving forward.

To those whose lives I've touched around the world.

CONTENTS

INTRODUCTION:

Woman to Woman

First Ladies, as the wives of our country's presidents are known, have often shared their husbands' platform of power to address causes close to their hearts. In recent times you might think of Hillary Clinton's advocacy for children's rights or Laura Bush's passion for literacy. Thrust into a national spotlight, these strong women often discover opportunities to help those in need, to create programs and solicit aid for special causes.

My husband, Bishop T. D. Jakes, lovingly refers to me as his First Lady, and has uniquely encouraged my special gifts in ministry here at our church, The Potter's House, and around the world. I continue to be humbled by the opportunities God affords me to speak, lead, and pray in a variety of settings. While numerous ministries spark my compassion, none capture my heart more than sharing the liberating truth of the gospel with hurting women. Single women, married women, teens, and those saints in their later years; successful businesswomen and stay-at-home moms; the widowed, the single mothers; those abused and hurting, those whose lives have left them desolate and afraid to hope. Women who shine on the outside with successful careers and beautiful families but whose lonely souls ache. All of these are the women who burden my heart, for I am one of them.

You see, I minister not as some Wonder Woman who's achieved sainthood, but as a sister alongside you on the journey. A woman, a daughter, a wife, a mother—all part of who I am but not too far removed from what my husband calls my girl's heart. I know what it's like to be surprised by the unexpected joy of a friend's love and devastated by the loss of a parent. I've birthed some dreams and seen others shattered in the cracks of a broken heart.

Through my experiences and the lives of other women with whom I've been privileged to share confidences, I've examined dozens of issues that affect us inside, at the core of our identities: our childhoods, our parents, our dreams, our failures, our longings, our disappointments. Out of these various threads of our life's fabric, one bold pattern emerges in every woman's life. Put simply: the men in our lives.

Now before you think I'm about to play the blame game (which can be tempting at times but ultimately self-defeating) and before you think I'm going to diminish the power of a woman by saying she needs a man's approval (also tempting, but untrue, as proved by so many successful women in our world today), please listen. The issues surrounding the men in a woman's life often remind me of spokes on a wheel. If a woman's relationships with men are strong and healthy, then the spokes provide solid support and reinforcement from the hub or core of the woman's identity to the outlying rim of her influence in the world.

However, if spokes are broken or missing, the wheel's center often lacks the reinforcement it needs. The wheel falters like a flat tire on a speeding car and ends up in a ditch, broken by life's obstacles.

I believe if most of us are honest, we know the men in our lives have had a profound impact on how we view ourselves and our relationships with those around us. Most important, the men in our lives also shape our views of our Lord.

You may be saying to yourself, *Serita, this is the twenty-first century! I've raised children by myself, gone back to school, started my own business, established myself in a good career. I don't need men to tell me I'm strong and successful.* Perhaps all true, dear sister. Certainly in this new century there are more opportunities for women than ever before. Standing on the shoulders of our mothers and grandmothers and great-grandmothers, we have come such a long, long way. When my daughters tell me they might be a doctor or an engineer or an attorney, I know it's within their grasp.

But I also know a little about human nature, about the longings of a woman's heart, and about how our heavenly Father created us. I know, no matter how successful a woman may become, she still longs for her daddy's approval. No matter how much money she makes, how many degrees she has, how many children she raises, some part of her soul still aches for the loving comfort of strong male arms around her. It's part of what it means to be a woman.

With the power of these relationships in mind, I'd like to shine the spotlight on several men who play key roles throughout various seasons of our lives. Perhaps you've heard the old saying: "Behind every good man stands a good woman." My mother used to say it to me when pointing out the successful men in our church. It was often a way to give credit to a woman in an age when some men wouldn't admit their need for an equal partner. If we were to revise that saying for today, I believe it might go, "*Beside* every good man stands a good woman." Yes, we have made progress, ladies, and so have our men. We can now proudly proclaim, "I stand beside him" as strong, capable women.

In fact, the Lord created us this way. While God created unique and special differences in women and men, He created us every bit as equal to men and imparted to us special aspects of His identity. "Male and female He created them" (Genesis 1:27). We are precious reflections of our Creator's image. And we are designed to interact with the other half of His creation.

Certainly what we need from and give to the men in our lives varies with the seasons of our lives and the roles we play. It's different for a young girl looking up into her father's eyes than it is for a young woman seeing herself in the eyes of her boyfriend. It's different for a woman standing alongside her husband at the altar than it is for the woman standing next to her boss in the boardroom. Yet all of these interactions affect who we are and how we see ourselves, and this is the territory I'd like us to explore together in these pages.

Beside Every Good Man covers four sections, each one focusing on a different way a woman stands in her relationship to men and the consequent ways she sees herself. While I realize these seasons often vary in individual lives, in duration, and in complexity, I've also found from counseling many women and speaking to thousands more around the world that most women experience such seasons in their lives.

First, we'll explore what it means to grow up female and how we learned to be the women we are—both the positive and negative messages that were imparted. We'll look into the mirror and see ourselves again with the naïveté and tenderness of the girls we once were. We'll consider our relationships with our fathers and grandfathers, whether or not they anointed and affirmed us as God intended. We'll reflect on what our brothers and male peers taught us about our femininity by looking at how they protected and privileged us, or failed to do so, and how this shapes the men to whom we're attracted. Finally, in this section we'll admit any secrets from our past and lay them before the Healer who loves us best.

Next, romantic relationships come into focus as we explore what it means to be single without despair. We'll ask ourselves, *How do I maintain my strength and security without denying my hope for a relationship? How do I recognize the right man when he comes along?* I'll explain why I think we need to be both cherished and challenged by such a man. Then we'll look at ourselves through the eyes of these special men in our lives and uncover the subtle and not so subtle messages about who we are, what we expect, how we experience intimacy, and how we communicate differently as men and women. We'll conclude here by focusing on how our faith forms a permanent foundation upon which to build a loving future.

From here, we'll consider more of what it means to stand next to the leading man in our life and share the spotlight onstage together. And we'll ask ourselves, *What kind of leading lady do I want to be? What is the story I'm acting out on the stage of my life?* As many of us have experienced, the fierce demands of motherhood, career, and homemaking often leave little time for romance and passion, so how do we maintain our relationship at the heart of it all?

We'll stop the juggling act for a moment and rest our weary souls long enough to see the bigger picture and hear the still, small voice of our Lord's calling. We'll consider how this calling affects our relationships to others in our lives: our children, our bosses and coworkers, our employees, our pastors, and friends.

In this book's final section, we'll reconsider what it means to look at ourselves after life events have brought the change of loss to our souls. Whether it's divorce or death, the infidelity of a spouse, the rebellion of a beloved child, a lost job or postponed dream, we all have life disappointments that gnaw at our well-being. How do we overcome these obstacles and endure as wise and joyful women? How do we take care of ourselves when our heart is breaking? We'll define true maturity and consider how we can survive our losses without losing faith. We'll look for mentors, those wise women ahead of us, as well as begin looking for opportunities to mentor other women in need. We'll conclude by seeing ourselves anew through our Creator's eyes, finding the confidence, in His love for us and our love for ourselves, to resume living to the fullest.

And throughout all these sections, as we address these seasons and our various relationships to men, I'll share some of my journey with you. I'll confide in you, woman to woman, without pretending to have all the answers. More important, I'll share what I see in God's Word about what it means to be created in a divine image and about how God wants us to relate to the men in our lives. My hope after we've spent this time together is that you can stand with that paradox of pride and humility, of meekness and strength, of compassion and courage, that identifies each of us not just as a woman, but as a Lady.

PART 1

I Stand Without Him: Seeing Yourself in the Mirror

Alone but Not Alone:
Our Heart's Mirror

Have you ever held a baby before a mirror so she could see herself? She coos and points, laughs and makes faces at the eager child just on the other side of the glass. I treasure the memories of holding each of my children in my arms, lifting the little one to catch sight of his or her reflection for the first time. Perhaps you have experienced this with your own children, a younger brother or sister, or your niece and nephew. There's a sense of amazement at the sight of a baby seeing herself for the first time. She may not even realize it's herself she's looking at. One of my own daughters would point at her own reflection and say, "I see baby!" never identifying that sweet smile as her own. It was only after I said her name, pointed to her image in the glass, and then back to her that she began to make the connection.

Now think for a moment. When was the last time you looked yourself in the eye? This morning when you were putting on makeup? In the ladies' room after lunch? In the rearview mirror when driving the car pool? As you rushed past the store window and caught your reflection from the sidewalk? And what did you see, dear sister, as you looked in the mirror at yourself? I pray that you were able to smile and see the beauty and confidence of a joyful woman who knows the Lord's peace. But from my own experiences, as well as those of other women, I know this might not have been the case.

Instead of greeting ourselves and holding our heads high, we ladies often immediately glare and criticize: *If only my eyes were a little wider, my lashes a little longer. If only my cheeks were a little higher and my lips a bit fuller. If I only could lose some weight. If I could afford that new designer face cream.* Or if not criticism, we sometimes can't even look ourselves in the eye because of past shame, present grief, or future worry. For most of us, the joyful exuberance of a baby seeing herself in the mirror for the first time has long since evaporated.

Our Heart's Reflection

Please don't misunderstand. It's not that I think we should be overly concerned with our appearances for the sake of vanity. Our culture certainly pressures us enough to be obsessed with looking younger, prettier, and sexier without my adding to it. No, I want us to look beyond the image we see in the glass. I want us to consider our heart's reflections so we can know where we are as we begin this journey together through these pages. There's something essential about knowing where you are that's helpful and necessary in planning where you're going next. I'll never forget my delighted frustration when my husband planned a surprise vacation for us and wouldn't tell me what kind of climate we would find awaiting us. I didn't know whether to take my raincoat or my swimsuit! I want us to know where we are so we can anticipate where we are going.

So we begin now by considering what has happened between that first glimpse of ourselves in the mirror when we were babies and who we are now as grown women. We do this not to become self-absorbed and preoccupied with ourselves but to have a greater understanding of who we are now and what our heart desires. I choose this starting point because it reflects so much of my own experience on my life's journey. Before I can consider my relationships with the men in my life, I must stand alone. And by standing alone I realize I am never alone; my Creator, the Lover of my soul, has been there beside me throughout it all. Therefore, we will look at ourselves, alone but not alone, so we may know where we are, but also so we may sense God's presence throughout our lives.

As I counsel and minister to numerous and various women from all walks of life, I discover that my issues concern them also. We want to explore and enhance our identities as women, our relationship to God, and our relationship to the men in our lives. We want to grow closer to the Lord, to be stronger and surer of who we are and how God has gifted us. We want to be closer to the men in our lives, from our father and brothers to our husband and sons, and know how to give ourselves to these relationships without losing ourselves in the process. We will cover these issues together in the following chapters.

Before we continue, allow me to address one other concern you may have. You may be asking yourself, *Why is Serita qualified to walk with me on my journey? When did she get it all figured out?* Please let me assure you, I don't have all the answers. Certainly I am no expert on male-female relationships. I'm not a psychologist or professional counselor, not a marriage therapist or relationship guru. But I am a woman blessed with a few glimmers of insight into how these three areas are intricately interwoven like the finest garment clothing a woman's life. I have lived as a daughter, sister, single woman, wife, lover, mother, and friend. I have studied the Scriptures and committed myself before the Lord to discover who He has created me to be and how I am to relate to those around me. I have learned from other women both gracious and courageous enough to reveal their true selves. Please allow me the privilege of sharing my heart, my study of God's Word, and the seeds of wisdom the Lord has bestowed upon me.

Masterpiece in the Making

Let's begin by being honest about where we are right now. If I may gently guide you to stand before the mirror of your heart, what do you see? What has transpired in life between the hint of a baby girl's smile that lingers from so long ago and the latest tiny wrinkle near your eyes? Who looks back at you?

As we attempt to consider who we are and where we are at this stage in our journey, two obstacles often obscure the image before us. Like a fog rolling in and hiding the stars, we lose sight of our purpose and the light our God wants to shine through us. The first of these obstacles results from being *nearsighted*. We become so immersed in the daily details of working, cooking, shopping, cleaning, and paying the bills that we lose perspective. Like a nearsighted person, we can't see things at a distance, only up close. But this creates a problem in that we can't see the proverbial forest of our lives for the immediacy of all the trees. When we lose a larger sense of purpose in our lives, then it's hard to stay motivated each morning when we wake up.

I believe the image we see of ourselves is not so much a reflection but a collage of hundreds of our reflections over time. It's as if a divine portrait painter has captured our image, with each detail and brush stroke revealing something of who we are and what we've experienced. See that line of color there? That's the blush of joy from your father's praise when you were four years old. And that delicate brush stroke near your lips? That's the faint scar from being overlooked by the boy you liked in junior high.

So many memories and moments of your lifetime. These bits of your life may be visible to no one but yourself, hidden beneath your flawless complexion and dazzling smile, camouflaged by foundation and blush, powder and mascara. Or some faint battle scars may grace your face and signal to others that you have endured and survived many hardships, many trials. Perhaps the truth about yourself is hardest to hide in your eyes, the mirrors of the soul.

Look again into your heart's mirror. As you stand alone now before yourself, what do you see? Regardless of whether or not the brush strokes of your lifetime are visible to those around you, can you see the accumulated beauty of an impressionistic painting? Step back. Can you see the larger frame of God's love around yourself? When you stand close to one of the great masters of impressionism such as Monet, the painting looks almost abstract, random steaks of color intersecting on the canvas. However, seen from a distance across the gallery, the rectangle of color captures the intricacies of a beautiful floral scene, a garden bursting with purple blossoms beside a serene pond of green lily pads.

Can you see the masterpiece God is creating in your life? I

believe the psalmist well described this process of stepping back and taking in God's masterpiece:

> For You formed my inward parts;
> You covered me in my mother's womb.
> I will praise You, for I am fearfully and wonderfully made;
> Marvelous are Your works,
> And that my soul knows very well. (Psalm 139:13–14)

All too often, I'm afraid, we lose sight of God's marvelous handiwork, His purpose and design, in the colorful canvas of our lives. We get so caught up in the everyday demands on our time and the numerous roles we must play that we lose sight of the girl alone in the mirror. That's when we must remind ourselves to pause once again and look at our heart's reflection. One of the Scripture verses that mean so much to me reminds me of this very need to refocus and see anew what God is doing in my life. "In returning and rest you shall be saved; in quietness and confidence shall be your strength," writes the prophet Isaiah (30:15). Pause for a moment where you are right now, sister, and let yourself rest before Him. Take a deep breath and let His peace envelop your heart before we go deeper and examine who we are and how we relate to the men in our lives. Perhaps you can pray the following prayer or use it as a model to express the intent of your heart:

———————————— ❧ ————————————

Lord, You are my Creator and the Divine Artist of my life. I ask You to help me see the beauty of Your brush strokes as I look back on my life and consider where You have brought me. Allow me to see beyond the nearsighted view of all my chores and responsibilities. Give me

Your perspective so I may see the masterpiece You are painting through my life. Amen.

———————————————— ⌒⌒ ————————————————

Fear Factor

Have you seen the television program where people compete for prizes by facing a variety of terrifying stunts? My teenage children begged me to watch it with them once, and I was repulsed by the numerous ways the contestants faced their fears. They ranged from skydiving to facing all kinds of creepy creatures. One poor woman let spiders crawl all over her!

I don't believe we have to go on "reality" television to face our fears, for the other obstacle that keeps us from seeing ourselves is indeed *fear.* We are afraid to look at ourselves for fear we might not like what we see. In fact, it's sometimes easier to stay caught up in the busy schedules and demanding roles than it is to slow down and look at yourself. Painful emotions may be waiting to pounce on you. You may not be able to look into your own eyes without seeing shame from past abuse or grief over your heart's losses. Perhaps you have lost a parent or one of your own children to the power of an addiction. You may feel haunted by the consequences of poor choices. Even amid the many relationships in your life, the loneliness of your soul may feel unbearable.

But even as you feel afraid, you must remember you are not alone and have never been alone. You must realize God's perfect love casts out all fear: "There is no fear in love; but perfect love casts out fear" (1 John 4:18). This truth cannot make your feelings instantly evaporate, but it can ground you in something stronger and larger than whatever fears may be preying on you. One way to dispel these fears is to realize you have survived this far by the grace of God, and He will not abandon you now. He tells us, "I will never desert you, nor will I ever forsake you" (Hebrews 13:5 NASB).

Pray for courage, dear lady, and for God's assurance to fill your heart with confidence. Ask Him to dispel the fears of the past, the stress of the present, and the worries of the future as you embark on this assessment. You may want to use the following prayer as a way to express this desire of your heart:

Dear Soul Keeper, I ask You to banish the fears from my heart. Please remind me of Your presence so I may consider how to grow closer to You, how to see more clearly what I need to change so that I may love You and those around me more fully. Give me courage and strength to face whatever past issues need to be addressed. Give me peace to see Your hand in my present circumstances. Give me hope to trust in Your plans for my future. Amen.

Cinderella at the Ball

When I was a girl growing up in West Virginia, my cousins and I loved to play in my auntie's closet. We would go through her old cedar chest and find discarded dresses and old-fashioned finery. We thrilled to see ourselves in beautiful floral prints and hats with fine feathers. A broken pearl necklace became royal treasure, and clip-on earrings glinted like prized diamonds. We called this game "Cinderella Dress-up" and never questioned how all of us could be Cinderella at the same time. We were too busy getting ready for the ball! There was room for each of us to have her own palace, and apparently her own respective Prince Charming (although boys were not our concern at the time).

The point was the joy of limitless possibility. We could each be a fairy princess, could be anything we wanted to be and do anything we wanted to do! We were princesses waiting to be discovered. Maybe we developed this silly, sweet game from hearing too many fairy tales or from watching one too many Disney films. But I'll never forget my soul's unfettered joy as my cousins and I giggled in front of the mirror, believing anything was possible and knowing happiness awaited us in a chest of old dresses. Perhaps you had a similar game when you were growing up. Maybe playing sports or collecting dolls afforded you this kind of childlike hope and magic. Maybe you found it in the books you read or the stories you heard.

As we stand alone gazing at our heart's reflection, I believe it's important that we rekindle this innocent passion for several reasons. We not only want to assess where we have come from and realize that we are not alone; in addition, we need to reconnect with the early dreams of our girl's hearts. We do this not for reasons of nostalgia, a wistful remembrance of the "good old days," but as a way of remembering the power of possibility, a way of reconnecting to where we are going. Our dreams, like a bouquet of balloons, brought us joy . . . until the harsh winds of life snatched them away. We must reclaim those brightly colored dreams of girlhood and make them anchors for where we are going. For there's often something honest and authentic about those dreams. If we want to rediscover who we truly are and what has shaped us, then I believe we must look at those early hopes and joys. Somewhere within each of us is the girl who continues to dream. She may be bruised and battered; she may have a gag in her mouth so she cannot whisper into your soul. But she is there, dear sister, longing to be set free again. Can you see her playing dress-up in her mama's long dress? Can you hear her singing a simple song?

Before you dismiss this as foolishness, please consider that it's often our childhood dreams that guide our successes in the present. I was reminded of this while watching the 2002 Academy Awards. Halle Berry became the first African-American woman to win the Oscar for Best Actress. (In fact, Denzel Washington won that same night for Best Actor.) Ms. Berry's acceptance speech was especially memorable, bringing me to share her tears as she thanked the numerous pioneers before her: Lena Horne, Eartha Kitt, Alfre Woodard, and Ruby Dee. She concluded by sharing how her girlhood dreams had kept her persevering and striving toward the achievement for which she was recognized that night.

The moment caused me to reflect on my own life and the many blessings the Lord has bestowed on me: the love of a special husband who is fulfilling his calling, beautiful children, my health, a wonderful home in which to nurture our family, a platform of ministry to other women, and special friendships with dear sisters. I considered the incredible privilege I've enjoyed to speak to various and diverse women, from society women to welfare mothers, business executives to homemakers, teenage mothers to great-grandmothers. In many ways the Lord has blessed me more than any fairy godmother ever blessed Cinderella. He has made me His princess, His leading lady. Similarly, I believe He desires for each one of us to discover our identity as His royal daughter.

The obstacles, however, are legion. In spite of the out-pouring of His blessings on my life, it is far from perfect. My joy in His purposes for my life has not been without sacrifice, considerable pain, and shattered dreams along the way. I've lost both my parents to dreadful diseases. I've waited in the emergency room over the injuries of my children. I've endured a terrible car accident that left me wondering if I would ever walk again. I've suffered the betrayal of women I once trusted. Even in my childhood game of Cinderella, the clock struck twelve and the ball was over.

Similarly, I recall hearing Ms. Berry speak about all the parts she hadn't gotten because of directors' prejudices and their misperceptions of her. No, it's not easy to hold on to our dreams. It's not easy to look at our reflection in the mirror and consider the composite portrait of who we have become. It re-quires honesty, courage, and humility. We have to be willing to look at ourselves alone, through no one else's eyes, no one else's expectations. We each have to find our own path and seek the Lord's wisdom on our life's journey.

Perhaps you're thinking it's too late, that too many changes have occurred in your life for you to begin again. These changes may seem especially clear in your relationships with the men in your life: too many words said in haste or anger, too many words left unsaid, too many acts to be forgiven on both accounts. Or you may feel it's too painful to stir up the dreams of your girlhood, that you'd only be stirring up mem-ories and hopes that were forced to die long ago. Maybe you feel the ashes are so cold there are no sparks of life left from which to kindle a new fire. You once wanted to start your own business or pursue your love of music or become a teacher, but you're afraid there's too much time and heartache between your past and your present.

If you find yourself in this swirl of disappointment and uncertainty, I invite you to claim the truth of God's Word and remember how much He delights in blessing us as His children and restoring us. It's like when my children were younger and would come in from playing outside with their jeans muddy and T-shirts tattered, their arms scraped and faces dirty. Can you guess my first inclination? Yes, you're right! I couldn't wait to get them into the bathtub and then into clean clothes. I wanted to bandage any cuts and scrapes and wipe away any tears. Often I would be reminded of a verse in Scripture: "If you then, being evil, know how to give good gifts to your children, how much more will your Father who is in heaven give good things to those who ask Him!" (Matthew 7:11). How true this is! Nothing is impossible with our God, so don't be afraid to muster your seed of faith and reconsider your dreams, desires, and destiny.

I hope you, dear reader, are actively pursuing your dreams—growing in your awareness of who you are and how God made you, striving for excellence in the pursuit of your calling, and standing strong next to the men in your life. I applaud your journey and hope you will find continued nourishment for your dreams and preventive insight into how you relate with men. May you continue to grow and flourish so God can work His masterpiece in your life.

Regardless of where you are in your life, whether or not you can touch the fabric of your dreams or only view it from a distance, whether there's a key man in your life or not, I encourage you to reflect upon who you see in your heart's mirror. Be as brutally honest as you can about who you truly are and what you honestly need. Don't beat yourself up for past mistakes or linger on the scars and age lines. Instead, give thanks and bask in the beauty that is there in your eyes, in your heart, as you prepare to embark on a journey of self-discovery, greater intimacy with God, and stronger strides with the men in your life.

Before we continue by looking at other forces that have shaped us, I encourage you to linger here before your heart's mirror as long as you need. Drink in the beauty of the Lord's presence in your life this far. Stand before yourself, knowing you are not alone. Dispel the busyness and fear that would so easily entangle you on your path. Reconnect to your girlhood dreams. Consider where you are going. And let the journey begin!

———————————————— ⟨⟩ ————————————————

Dear God, I'm scared and excited as I begin this journey. Please give me the courage to look myself in the eye and to seek Your truth. I pray I would be honest about the barriers in my life that keep me from loving myself and from loving the men in my life. Give me Your divine strength and a willingness to lean on You as the source of healing for broken areas of my life. Be my guide, the Lover of my soul, my Secret Keeper, and the One who stands beside me through all the seasons of my life. Amen.

———————————————— ⟨⟩ ————————————————

Questions and Suggestions

1. Why did you pick up this book? What question or thought in this chapter struck a chord with you as you began to think about who we are and how you relate to men?

2. How would you describe the present season of your life? Busy? Hectic? Complicated? Relaxing? Painful? Hopeful? What are your goals for this season? In other words, what kinds of changes would you like to see in your life and in yourself?

3. Do something creative to express how you see yourself at present. It may be writing a poem, drawing a picture, painting your self portrait, cooking your favorite dish, or creating a collage. You don't have to share it with anyone and you don't have to be Martha Stewart to do it.

4. Consider keeping a journal to record your thoughts and feelings as you read each chapter in the book. Use this as a safe place to process your life and faith. You may want to address some of your entries to God as written prayers.

5. Who are your role models and inspirations? How do these women encourage you to strive for more? What is it about them that you would like to emulate in your life?

6. Commit yourself to praying about the specific areas and relationships in your life where you would like to grow. You might use the prayers provided in each chapter as a way to get started.

Playing House, Part 1:
The Love of Our Father

Can you remember playing house as a little girl? I sure can. My cousins and I would sit underneath the kitchen table with our favorite dolls and dress-up clothes. We'd make my baby brother be the daddy and send him off to work while we pretended to cook and clean for his return. He'd go into the next room, often to complain to our auntie about having to play with us girls, and then reluctantly rejoin us in our "house." I'd wear my aunt's apron and produce a pie tin with an imaginary apple pie or plate of corn bread. What great fun it seemed to flirt with the grown-up world while remaining firmly grounded in the carefree innocence of childhood. There were no rules or set objectives; we were simply playing house based on our observations of the ways our own home was run.

Still today, even with all the fancy electronic toys and sophisticated computer games, little girls love to play house. It's a way for children to connect with parents and their world, to imitate their role models and experiment with perceptions of their responsibilities. This can be a dangerous thing sometimes. I remember a friend telling me that her three-year-old daughter would play house by sending her older brother outside to do yard work while she talked on the phone and watched TV "just like Mom"!

Rules of Roles

Amazingly, for a childhood game that has no rules, we sure do take away a lot of them. For out of this imitative play, based on what we observe of our own parents and household, ideas emerge about what it means to be female and male. Growing up when I did, most women stayed home and tended to the children and the homemaking chores. Most men in our neighborhood worked in the coal mine or in construction or in a business in a nearby town, which kept them away from the house during the day. When the men came home, the women were expected to wait on them and serve them. In return, the men provided a paycheck to keep the bills paid and food on the table.

You may have experienced similar "rules" about gender roles. Or you may have grown up with roles radically different from what I describe that nonetheless carried firm expectations. Perhaps you've already reflected on the messages you took from childhood about what it means to be female and a wife or mother, about what you want your man to be like, about how you want the roles divided in your own home. If you have, now is a good time to examine the connections between these messages and the woman you've become. If you haven't considered them before, now is the perfect time to begin understanding the expectations shaping your life as a woman.

It's important to consider how we've been conditioned by

our upbringing so we can see who we really are. Often we maintain rules gleaned from our parents that are culturally imposed and not reflections of our Creator's design. Have you heard the story of the woman who was teaching her teenage daughter how to cook the Thanksgiving turkey?

"Now before you put it in the oven, you need to cut off about three inches from the end of the bird," said the woman.

"But why, Mama?" asked the daughter. "What does that do?"

The woman looked puzzled and shook her head. "I don't know," she replied. "It's just the way Mama always cooked the turkey. Let's call her and find out."

The woman called her mama and asked her the same question her daughter had asked her. "Well, I'm not sure," the older woman said over the phone. "Your grandma taught me to do it that way. Why don't you call her and ask her."

So the woman phoned her grandmother and posed the same question about why they needed to cut three inches off the Thanksgiving turkey. The old woman cackled with laughter. "Why, child," she said, "I always cut off the end of my turkey because my roasting pan wasn't big enough to hold that big old bird!"

Perhaps you have traditions or perceptions about your own identity that are just as useless and outdated. They may have served your mother or grandmother for a specific purpose, but you no longer need to carry them with you today. Whether you were aware or not before of the rules and the roles you play, you must now examine them and ask yourself why you're still cutting off the turkey when you have bigger pans today! Before you continue, consider the following prayer to help you begin this process of looking closer at your own game of "playing house."

———————————— ∽ ————————————

Dear Lord, so many factors have shaped who I am. Help me to consider the various messages from my upbringing and discard the ones that are not part of Your design for me. Give me eyes to see, dear Father, so that I may rise above what is outdated or no longer useful in my perceptions of what it means to be a woman. Give me courage and wisdom to know what is from You as I continue forward on my journey. Amen.

———————————— ∽ ————————————

Coal Miner's Daughter

As we reflect on how our parents shaped our identities and the ways we relate to the men in our lives, one of the first places we must look is at our relationship with our earthly father. Certainly, we can't cover all the complex ways our parents influenced our views, but we can address some of their major contributions. We'll save the relationship with our mother and how she influenced us for the next chapter. For now, please allow me to share some of my relationship with my father so you may see his influence upon me. So much of who I am and how I relate to my brothers, my husband, and my sons comes from this relationship with the first man in my life.

My father was a coal miner in West Virginia, one of those men whose lives were spent digging underground in dark caves to produce that precious fuel source. Since Daddy was often gone for days at a time to earn a living for his family, I didn't see him as often as either of us would have liked. The memories I do hold of his presence in my life, however, are treasured in my heart. I can recall his strong hands combing my hair, brushing it, smoothing it flat against my head, then brushing it some more, gently and tenderly. I recall the way he smelled like clean cedar and tobacco, the scent of earth lingering from his time in the coal mine.

Similarly, I can remember intimate moments simply sitting on his lap and resting against his chest. His heart beat just inches from my ear, and the soft drumming was such a comfort. It's no wonder infants are often quieted by the sound of a human heartbeat. The closeness, the rhythm of life coursing between parent and child, was like an unspoken language between my father and me.

In addition to these sweet moments of intimacy, other indelible memories unfold in my mind. I recall Daddy cracking fresh coconuts for the Christmas cakes Mama would bake. I remember him taking me to a local carnival. Certainly it was nothing like Six Flags or the amusement parks of today—merely a traveling caravan of red tents and colorful rides—but it was special to me. Daddy would wait patiently while I rode the carousel, waving at me each time I passed by as if it were my first.

Painful memories emerge as well. Daddy suffered a broken back from an accident in the mine and was bedridden for months, told he'd never walk again. He did walk again, and I can see him slowly shuffling around. He always wore his favorite ball cap, and I can picture him watching a baseball game or talking sports with his buddies. Even today when I see my own sons wearing a ball cap, I think of him.

Later Daddy contracted black lung disease, another toll of working the mines his whole life. Even as I knew he was dying,

I couldn't get my mind around the loss of his presence in my life. I recall doing my elementary school science project on black lung disease, as if my understanding of the terrible infliction would bring me closer to him, would allow me to prevent the disease from constricting the flow of air through his lungs.

When I lost him, it was late evening in the middle of autumn. What started as a warm, crisp day turned dramatically cooler. Although the leaves pulsed with red and gold, their colors looked dull before my sorrowful eyes. The day after he died, I went to school and tried to act as if nothing had happened. Mama and my family were so caught up in their own grief and preparations for the funeral that no one thought to keep me home. But sitting in my eighth-grade math class, I could no longer fight back the tears. One of my friends asked and I shared the cause of my sadness. She told our teacher, who then kindly ushered me out of the classroom and helped me prepare to go home.

This story strikes me as significant because, you see, I didn't realize the impact losing my father would have on my life. Perhaps it was childish denial to avoid the tender wound of such a loss, or maybe I hoped it wouldn't hurt me so much because I didn't see my father as often as I liked. Out of this loss and grief, however, I began to learn two important truths: The need for my daddy was greater and deeper than I ever realized, and his presence in my life greatly affected, and still affects, who I am today.

Papa's Power

Based on my counseling relationships and friendships with other women, I am not alone in experiencing these truths. Our relationship with our father goes a long way in shaping how we learn to feel loved and cared for, to feel secure and safe. If we lose our father at an early age, as I did, or if he abandoned us or harmed us, then our first major taste of pain in life may lie in this relationship. Regardless of where a father's presence falls on the spectrum—loving on one end to abusive on the other—he remains a key player in the drama of our lives. Our relationship with our dad dramatically influences how most of us first learn to relate to men in our lives and contributes to our first impression of God.

With the exception of losing him so early in my life, my relationship with my daddy falls on the positive end. And even after he passed away, I was blessed to have my uncle become a father figure for me. Many other women I know whose fathers were not present were similarly blessed to have a "village father" who loved them as a daughter and provided them with security and love.

However, on the other end of the spectrum, the wounds a woman experiences from her father can run very deep. Tragically, so many women have negative relationships marred by their father's verbal or physical abuse or by his absence. Instead of a loving protector who championed his little girl into becoming a glorious and godly woman, this father stunted his daughter's growth with shame, lack of self-esteem, and lack of healthy involvement in her life.

I recall a young woman who approached me after I spoke at a women's conference. Tall and slender, with wide eyes and a beautiful complexion, she moved toward me like a model (she was certainly dressed like one) and asked if she could speak with me in private. My talk at the conference had focused on our identity as holy women, and I assumed this lovely young woman wanted to share what the Lord was doing in her life.

Later over coffee, however, I learned my words troubled her greatly, for she didn't feel confident in her identity as a woman of God at all. When I commented on what a beautiful first impression she made, she smiled and cast down her eyes. "I'm faking it. I may look like a grown woman on the outside—I know how to dress and what to do—but I still feel like a little girl on the inside. So afraid and vulnerable. It's silly, I know," she tried to explain, "but I feel so scared most of the time. I hate making decisions for myself and can't stand to let others make them for me. And I'm attracted to the wrong kind of men. But that's another story. What's wrong with me, Sister Jakes?" Her poised control dissolved before me as tears coursed down her cheeks.

Numerous questions came to mind, but because we had so little time together, I asked if I could pray for her. She nodded and I held her hands and asked the Lord to bless this woman and set her free to be His daughter whom He loved and had created for special purposes. During the prayer, I addressed God as our Abba Father, our Daddy, as the apostle Paul instructs us in Romans: "For you did not receive the spirit of bondage again to fear, but you received the Spirit of adoption by whom we cry out, 'Abba, Father'" (8:15). At this reference, the young woman sobbed even more, and I sensed she had suffered some deep wound connected to her earthly father.

After our prayer I asked her about her parents. Her tears subsided a bit, and she relayed that her father had left her mother when she was a toddler and was later killed in a car accident. Her mother remarried, and her stepfather was abusive and cruel. He had molested this young woman into her teen years and constantly berated her with insults and contempt. She had received some counseling but found she still struggled with depression and anger over what this man had done to her and her siblings.

A father has such power in our lives, dear lady. His role is so essential, so vital, in our lives that one way or another we will be shaped by how he relates to us. And since there are no perfect people, it's likely that all of us carry some disappointments, some losses in our relationship with our daddy. Without him, we have no full sense of what it means to be different and special, to be loved and adored simply for who we are as precious daughters. And the power of a loving daddy—even one who is human and makes mistakes—cannot be underestimated. For he can give us the first glimpse into a heavenly Father who finds us beautiful, both inside and out.

Daddy's Girls

It's certainly no accident that God reveals Himself as a father figure again and again throughout Scripture. The psalmist called Him "a father of the fatherless" (68:5) and the prophet Isaiah wrote, "You, O LORD, are our Father; Our Redeemer from Everlasting is Your name" (Isaiah 63:16). So we're clearly encouraged to think of and relate to the Almighty as our heavenly Father. Why does this pose a problem? As we've already begun to uncover, this Divine Parent-earthly child relationship is complicated by our own frame of reference with our earthly father. Regardless of how much we might want to ignore or separate the man who fathered us from the reality of God as our Father, many of us cannot.

Down through the generations, many fathers have abused

their roles of leadership and loving service to their families. Instead of covering and protecting their children, they suffered their own weaknesses and fears onto their offspring. They ended up trying to manipulate and control their sons and daughters rather than empower them as God's precious creation.

Maybe you had a father who wanted to know where you were 24/7. He told you what you could and couldn't do, what you could wear, where you could go, what time to be home, and who you could go with. If you disobeyed, the punishments were harsh. But more than the punishments, perhaps it felt as though your father withheld his love if you didn't do exactly what he wanted. Like a rosebush with the threat of the sun being taken away, you feared that you couldn't exist without Daddy's approval. So you harbored anger and resentment until it festered into bitterness. You numbed your heart and pretended you didn't need Daddy's love, when in truth it remained vital to you, and the hurt was deep.

And now you wonder why you see God as a kind of supreme dictator. You find yourself attracted to legalistic churches with a complete list of do's and don'ts because it feels like home. As much as you hate it, you at least feel that you know how to please Daddy and earn his approval. Since your father ruled with an iron hand, you assume that God must also.

I have met many women who have come to The Potter's House after finally being disillusioned by the self-righteousness and hypocrisy of such a church. These women long to believe there's more to their lives than living out a checklist. Do they dare to believe that God loves them for who they are, created them for His divine purposes, with a blessed future ahead of them? The answer is a resounding Yes!

Part of the solution, my sister, is to examine the association between our earthly father and the Father of our lives. What many women discover is that they must acknowledge how their fathers failed them and separate the painful impact of these failures from the perfect Father—heart of the living God. One way to go about this is to consider the ways fathers originally served their families. Around the world, in a variety of cultural settings and time periods, the father's power was usually intended to protect and serve his children. He would use his physical strength to protect his family from wild animals, thieves, and the elements of nature. He would use his resources to provide for his family, to give them shelter and food.

This is the kind of Father we have in our lives still—One who loves and serves and protects us. While God is certainly all-powerful and all-righteous, He uses His power to love and redeem us, not to condemn us. As I mentioned earlier, the apostle Paul encourages us to think of the God of the universe as a child might think of her daddy. How do we reprogram this view of God when our hearts remain heavy and soiled with the past of a less-than-perfect father?

It takes time, dear sister. But we cannot ignore the father-Father connection. We can't pretend we don't have issues with our earthly fathers when we do. We can't deny we don't need his presence in our lives or that he didn't affect who we are and how we live our lives. Have you observed a new father, perhaps in the hospital delivery room or days after the baby comes home? I'll never forget my husband's expression of sheer, astonished joy each time he held one of our newborn children in his arms for the first time. Why, he looked like a drunken man, he was so infatuated with those babies! I'm truly blessed, I know, for my awareness of God's love for me as His daughter has grown and blossomed by observing what a good father my husband is.

I'll never forget when our first daughter was three months old and my husband took her to the doctor. She had been listless and colicky, crying and obviously uncomfortable. He offered to take her to the doctor so I could rest after two long nights up with her, and so I could spend some time with our boys. I expected him to return in a couple of hours with a prescription or some baby aspirin. Instead, he called me from the hospital. Our daughter had been admitted immediately; she was dehydrated and suffering from some virus the doctor couldn't identify at present. The concern in his voice was so thick across the phone, I could tell he was scared. I could tell how much he loved his little girl and wanted her to be well.

After several excruciating days, our daughter improved and was released, but I'll never forget how seeing her father's concern brought me new insight into God's concern for me. It touched me deeply and gave me a new way to connect with my Abba Father, who loves me as His precious daughter. I know many of you have also experienced a similar, powerful revelation of God's tender Father-heart through the strong men in your life.

God also reveals His love to you directly. He dotes on you, dear sister. He loves you like no other. Will you let Him? I encourage you not only to think through the ways your earthly father may have contributed to negative views of God, but to look for the good ways he contributed as well, and the ways other men have revealed to you a father's love. And merely being aware is not enough for change. Ask God to show you His Father's heart toward you. One place to start is to consider how Jesus shows the love of His Father:

> Then they brought little children to Him, that He might touch them; but the disciples rebuked those who brought them. But when Jesus saw it, He was greatly displeased and said to them, "Let the little children come to Me, and do not forbid them; for of such is the kingdom of God. Assuredly, I say to you, whoever does not receive the kingdom of God as a little child will by no means enter it." And He took them up in His arms, laid His hands on them, and blessed them. (Mark 10:13–16)

Our Lord will never turn you away. You are His precious daughter, the apple of His eye. God always has time for His beloved children and wants to give us new ways of relating to Him as our Father. I encourage you to use the following prayer as a way of continuing your awareness of your Abba Father's love for you:

Dear Daddy, even as those words may be hard for me to say, I pray that You would reveal Yourself as my loving Father. Help me to see the associations I need to break between my earthly father's failures and my misperceptions of You. Enable me to forgive him these failures and release me from their impact. Help me to see all the positive ways my earthly father or village father demonstrated Your strength, Your service, and Your unconditional love for me. Bless me as Your daughter and hold me as Your child. Amen.

Questions and Suggestions

1. Can you recall "playing house" when you were a girl? What acts did you imitate from observing your parents and your own household? Do these messages remain in your life today?

2. What three key words would you use to describe your relationship with your father while you were growing up? Find three more key words to capture your relationship with him today.

3. What has remained the same in your relationship with your father from the time you were growing up until now? What has changed?

4. Write a letter to your father, whether he's living or dead, and tell him what's on your heart after reading this chapter. Be as honest as possible.

5. Make a list of things your father taught you about gender roles. You might label one column "Daddy taught me that men are . . ." and the other column "Daddy taught me that women should be . . ."

6. How has your relationship with your father shaped your views of God? Where is this most prevalent in your spiritual journey?

7. How has your relationship with your dad influenced what you look for in the other men in your life?

_๑ 3 ๑_

Playing House, Part 2: Mother of Our Hearts

Just as our fathers often shape our view of the heavenly Father, we may be most directly influenced in what we do and how we see ourselves by our mothers. If you think back to those games of dress-up and playing house when you were a girl, Mama most likely served as your role model. We acted out what we saw our mothers doing, whether cooking and cleaning and changing the baby, or working outside the home.

What we continue to discover is the extent to which we are still influenced by this most important woman in our lives. Many of the ways we see ourselves as a woman are shaped by our observations of our mother and her behavior. Indeed, the ways she related to the men in her life formed the blueprint for our later attempts. That's not to say we're doomed to forever repeat our mother's mistakes; however, her influence on how we view our father, and later the men we date and marry, is undeniable. Please allow me to share a few of the lessons I learned from observing my maternal role models.

Double Vision

I was privileged growing up to have a wonderful role model. My mother modeled many powerful strengths to me in the ways I observed her relate to both my father and other men in her life. She was beautiful, strong, and determined to make a better life for herself and her family. It was clear to me, in the ways they spoke kindly and showed affection, she and my father loved each other. As I look back now, I can see that the nature of their personalities made their marriage a bit unconventional. My father was quieter and more reactive to life's circumstances, while my mother was livelier and more proactive. Daddy waited on things to happen, while Mama believed you had to make things happen. I'm not sure at what point I realized this—perhaps after my father passed on—but they provided a lovely complement to each other. While I didn't acknowledge it during my teenage dating years, my parents' marriage eventually helped me realize that I wanted a complementary partner as well. As we will explore further in our next chapter, finding a man who complements your personality instead of one who competes with it is a worthy goal.

As I shared before, my daddy was a coal miner, hardworking and gentle in nature. Unusual for our small community, my mother worked outside the home, for small businesses in our nearby town or selling products to women door-to-door. She possessed an entrepreneurial spirit and always looked like a million dollars. In contrast to my father's overalls and work clothes, my mother wore beautiful suits and dresses and knew how to accessorize with colorful jewelry, purses, and shoes. She always smelled like a beautiful summer bouquet of the most exquisite flowers. Even as a child I realized how glamorous she was in comparison to other mothers in our neighborhood. I was so proud of her. She was confident and strong, and while she clearly loved my father, I never sensed that she needed his approval to know who she was.

She conveyed several important messages to me about being a female and relating to men. Not surprising considering her professional dress and appearance, I learned to relate to my body and looks based on what I observed from her. This was not an easy process. As I grew into my teenage years, my body changed rapidly, as all girls' bodies do. I wasn't very athletic, and my legs didn't seem to be growing as fast as my hips and fuller figure. I loved the sweet potato pies and chocolate cakes that Mama made, and the result probably didn't help me feel better about myself as I began to compare my appearance to the other girls in school. They all looked so beautiful, I thought. Why couldn't I look more like them, more like the thin models in *Seventeen* magazine? Why couldn't I even look more like Mama?

After an extended bout of exercise and severe dieting, I discovered that external beauty is not all it appears to be. My mother observed my discomfort with my appearance, along with my attempts to change it, before talking to me about inner beauty. At the time, her words sounded like one of those parental speeches that mothers recite to comfort their children. I wanted to look thinner and more glamorous, and she was lecturing me about my inner heart. It took years, but her words stayed with me. Beauty does, indeed, begin on the inside. One can have the looks of a supermodel, but without a genuine sense of worth, a confidence borne of being God's daughter, and a poise forged by accepting your own self, one will never possess true beauty. This may have been one of the most important lessons I learned from my mother.

A second strong maternal influence was my "village mama," my auntie, who was often my primary caretaker while my parents worked. Looking back, I see that my auntie lived out a more stereotypical role of homemaker and helpmeet to my uncle. She was a very down-to-earth woman who taught me many practical, domestic skills: how to clean, how to sew, how to make biscuits from scratch. Auntie kept a clean house and always had a meal waiting when her husband came home. She made many of her own clothes and had a plain and simple personal style, which often included an apron around her waist and thick-soled sensible shoes.

If my mother helped shape my view of myself as a woman, then my auntie instilled in me an awareness of how to create a home. She wasn't concerned about her house looking like a showplace—no one was back then. No, she paid attention to the details of comfort and practicality that would serve and delight her husband and us children. When my uncle arrived home after a too-long day, she welcomed him with a sincerity that transcended the hard day she may have had, too. She would embrace him, joke with him, lighten his load a little, making him aware that he was truly home. She cooked delicious food, remembered what everyone's favorite dish was, and always seemed to have a pie on hand when a neighbor dropped by unexpectedly. I learned to appreciate her hospitality and gracious spirit, her ability to create a home that was a safe and desirable place for her family. Later, as a single woman on my own, I realized how much I valued my auntie's gift for making a home and understood that whether single or married, I wanted to be like her: a catcher of beauty who shone a prism of rainbow light throughout my surroundings.

Supermodels

These two different women gave me a well-balanced view of how women functioned in the world at large. While my auntie certainly reinforced the more traditional, even stereotypical, model of femininity, she was not a weak, passive wallflower who needed a man to make her complete. She chose to serve my uncle, her children, and my family in ways that can only be described as a servant spirit of meekness and gentleness. Mama demonstrated that women did not have to stay at home and settle for less than their calling. In the midst of raising her family, she maintained her sales job and pursued her dreams of entrepreneurship.

As I grew older, married, and started raising my own family, my appreciation for these two remarkable women only escalated. I am truly blessed by their unique differences and contributions in my life. And as I've shared with friends and other women, I've realized that not all mothers impart as many positive lessons as mine did. Yes, our mothers and maternal figures are our primary role models—our first "supermodels" I call them—but sometimes their best attempts to help their daughters avoid their own mistakes can backfire. My dear friend's story comes to mind.

I'll call her Renee. She sauntered into the restaurant with a tall, attractive man hovering next to her. She obviously reveled in his attention and made a point to introduce him to me as her new man. He left her at my table with a passionate kiss and promised to pick her up as soon as she called him on his cell phone.

At first, I was happy for my friend; Renee was older than I but had never married. In fact, she never seemed to have the same boyfriend twice during our occasional lunches every few months. We chitchatted and caught up on our families and other mutual friends from back home. Then Renee began describing how she'd met Rodney at her church and how they'd been together for three months now. She clearly enjoyed this gentleman very much, but I could tell something was bothering her.

"So he could be husband material?" I asked with a smile.

"Oh, yes, Serita. I really think he could be the one. Only . . . Oh, nothing," she said and started to change the topic.

"What is it, Renee? What are you concerned about? He seems like a wonderful man—someone God has sent your way for a purpose."

"Yes, I really think so. Only, I haven't let him meet my mother yet . . ."

I asked after Renee's mother, also someone I had known growing up, and she filled me in. Then I returned to my friend's concern. "So does Mama have to approve in order for you to proceed with Rodney? You're a big girl now."

Renee's eyes began to mist. "That's just it, Serita," she said. "Mama has never thought any of the men in my life were good enough for me. You know what a rocky marriage my parents had. Daddy drank and couldn't hold a job. He ran around with other women. Sometimes I think he made Mama distrust *all* men. She's always warning me about not committing to a man and bringing up ways that Daddy hurt her as evidence for her case. Sometimes I think she's right: Men *are* bad news. Mama's just trying to protect me from all the heartache she's suffered. Maybe there's a good reason I haven't married yet."

As Renee and I continued our conversation, I was struck by how much my friend's mother had influenced the way she interacted with men. Here she was an attractive, grown woman over forty who still gave her mother much power over her own affairs of the heart. Similarly, she was even aware of being reluctant to trust men because of the dual impact of her father and her mother. In many ways, she was now modeling and reacting against the role she had watched her mother play all her life.

Indeed, our mothers are truly the first supermodels we encounter in life.

It's not that I don't think we shouldn't listen to our mothers. They usually have our best interests at heart and sometimes know us better than we know ourselves. But in talking with Renee, I realized that often our mother's baggage gets dumped into our trunk, and we're left driving around with extra weight that we don't need.

My Mama Told Me

As I reflected on other women friends besides Renee, as well as on the impact my own mother had on me, I realized that our mothers wield enormous power in how we view the opposite sex. Much of their advice is borne out of the hard-learned wisdom these older women have collected through heartache and disappointment. There's often good advice in waiting for the right man, in not rushing in and committing too quickly to our first infatuation. As I think back on some of my early

crushes and teenage boyfriends, I'm grateful for the caution-
ary wisdom my mother imparted. Like the song says, "My
mama told me, you better shop around!" But in Renee's case,
her mother's song had become a broken record. It seemed
clear that her mother's mistrust of Renee's father had caused
the older woman to impede her daughter's happiness.

As much as we love our moms, there comes a time when we
must grow up and stand on our own two feet, get in touch with
our heart, and ask ourselves what we really want in a man. We
have to pray earnestly and seek God's will in our lives, especially in this most important area of seeking a life partner. The
Scripture says it well: "When I was a child, I spoke as a child,
I understood as a child, I thought as a child; but when I became a *wo*man, I put away childish things" (1 Corinthians
13:11). Although the apostle Paul says "when I became a
man," I don't think he would mind my taking a small liberty
here to make this verse come alive for us ladies.

There comes a time in every woman's life when she must
pack away her girlish fantasies, her impossible expectations for
the perfect man, and her false hopes of being totally fulfilled if
only "the right man" would come along. In this same chest of
no-longer-useful-things, a woman must be willing to pack
away what her mother has slipped into the mixture, whatever
requisites and conclusions her mother developed about men
and passed on, either directly or indirectly. Put another way,
it's as if our mother saved her wedding gown for us, not realizing that the once beautiful dress has shrunk and clings way
too tightly on us. We have to find our own fit, perhaps keeping some of Mama's lace for our special dress, but not becoming inhibited by her garment of expectations. That's not to say
there isn't some of Mama's wisdom we should hold on to, but

we must sift through the messages she passed on to us. Let's examine some of the negative ways of relating to men that our mother may have telegraphed to us.

Learning by Example

As we've seen, so much of what we learn about how to relate to men we learn from our mothers and the other matriarchs in our early lives. We forget as adults how much children learn from us simply by watching and quietly observing, but if you think back, I'll bet you can remember some subtle and not so subtle messages you received from your mother and grandmother.

I recall recognizing an important lesson when I was older and had just broken up with a boyfriend. I felt alone and abandoned, wondering if anyone would ever find me attractive enough to ask out again. My self-image, like that of many teenage girls, was tied to being part of a couple, not standing on my own. After this particularly painful breakup, my mother stopped by my room at bedtime and prayed a soothing prayer: "Dear Father, help Serita to know her beauty apart from what any boy may think of her. Help her to know her worth as Your child and not as someone's girlfriend." Later, as I reflected on her loving words, I realized that even in the midst of being married to my father, my mother's confidence was all her own. As much as she loved my father, she didn't give him all the power to make her feel like a woman.

But this lesson is not always the first one many women learn from their mothers. Some women learn how to make a man jealous to get what they want. I recall a good friend of mine, whom I'll call Janelle, telling me that when she was a child, she always knew when her parents were fighting. Her mother would use extra makeup, spritz on the perfume, and wear flashier, more revealing, dresses. She would dress this way to go to the market, to the post office, even to church! When she returned, Janelle's father would accuse her of seeing another man or of being on the prowl for another man. Her mother would laugh and use her newfound power to get her point across, whatever it may have been.

As Janelle grew older, she realized that while her mother wasn't looking for another man, she was using her beauty and sex appeal to get what she wanted. If she had to make her man jealous to get what she wanted, then she would refine her looks into a bartering chip. If her husband would only grant what she wanted when he feared losing her, then so be it. Certainly not the best way to relate to your spouse, but a message Janelle had to consider as she wondered why so many of her boyfriends were often jealous, and why she often dressed and acted this way to keep them. She had learned to use her body as a commodity in relating to men.

"I basically disconnected my heart from the rest of myself and used my looks and my body to get what I wanted from the men in my life. No wonder they often resented me," Janelle told me later.

Too often in our mothers' generation, women held little power or respect socially or economically, so many learned to use what they had. Our fathers often bought into these cultural expectations and didn't grant our mothers the respect they deserved simply by nature of being God's child and their husbands' helpmeets. So they became manipulators. Whether that meant refusing to cook her husband's favorite stew or sleeping with her back to him, whether it was trying to make him jealous or lying to make him come home from the bar, our mothers did what they did to try to balance the distribution of power. It often worked.

Manipulation is such an unhealthy and undesirable way to relate, and I know you, like me, probably find it offensive. It goes against the core of feminine strengths such as gentleness and graciousness in ways that certainly do not please our Father or complement our men. However, the temptation to manipulate isn't reserved for strong-willed, overbearing mothers. Quiet and reserved ladies have often been just as guilty of manipulating their men. Many mothers may not have been so feisty and overt in trying to equalize their partnership with their husbands. You may have grown up with a quiet, demure mother . . . who may have been just as manipulative nonetheless. If your father controlled the relationship, as in the traditional patriarchal model of many American marriages, and your mother didn't overtly rebel, she may have learned to regain some control through passive resistance. Perhaps she felt direct communication was futile or that she couldn't stand to face constant conflict and confrontation. The husband became the antagonist and she outwardly placated him while inwardly seething.

This is the negative stereotype of the "little woman" who cooks, cleans, and delivers babies, all with a smile on her face and never a cross word. While it's tempting to think of this woman as a saint—and perhaps many are—often these smiling faces cover wells of bitterness and personal resentment. Women in my mother's generation were often afraid that their husbands would abandon, abuse, or ignore them if they didn't live up to their men's expectations, which were often falsely shaped by a cultural model that didn't exist. So they stifled their voices and quieted their hearts in order to maintain the status quo.

This passive attitude coating an interior anger can be incredibly dangerous. Certainly it's not always the cause of women's resigning themselves to domestic abuse or unhealthy relationships, but many daughters do grow up responding to men in ways they learned from their mothers. If their mothers never spoke up or expressed healthy boundaries, then these women have to learn them on their own.

Regardless of whether our mothers manipulated their husbands overtly or subtly, this way of relating tends to be defensive in nature rather than loving. When the marriage is like a chess match, women end up viewing men as the antagonist—their opponent. Since men would hurt or seek to rule, so they think, women do whatever it takes to maintain power by using their bodies, their services, or their compliance.

Our culture has certainly made progress in regard to providing equity between partners. Through the last decades of the twentieth century and into the twenty-first, more and more women have been regarded as equals to men. We have gained power through education and increased career opportunities and by supporting one another in the pursuit of our dreams. We have learned that we are not powerless and that our men respect and love us. Men who are seeking God's best for themselves and for those they love will not play this game either. They will seek to love and serve their women, not take power away because of their own insecurities.

Risky Business

Even when we know we're not powerless and are therefore not justifying our manipulation of men, we still sometimes struggle with wanting to control our relationships with men.

Whether Mama provided a prime example of how to do this or not, we're still selfish creatures when left to our own devices. We want our man to do what we want him to do! Just as he wants the same from us—it's human nature. "For all have sinned and fall short of the glory of God," the Scripture tells us (Romans 3:23).

I believe the desire to control and manipulate men may be a woman's area of greatest struggle. We want to be vulnerable and rest on his shoulder; we want to give our hearts and our bodies and know we are loved and cherished. But what danger! Loving someone is such risky business. We're asked to lay down our defenses, our own attempts to get what we want, and to offer our hearts, as tender and fragile as they may be. It's so much easier to protect ourselves and look for ways to take power where we find it and try to create a little insurance for ourselves.

In fact, if we think back upon our very first mother, this was the area in which she wrestled her greatest temptation. In the Garden of Eden, Adam and Eve knew a peace and harmony with each other and their Creator that none of us will ever know this side of heaven. The only rule, as you may recall, was to avoid the big, glistening tree in the center of the Garden— the Tree of the Knowledge of Good and Evil. But the evil one seized an opportunity to tempt the first wife by touching on her desire for more power:

> Now the serpent was more cunning than any beast of the field which the LORD God had made. And he said to the woman, "Has God indeed said, 'You shall not eat of every tree of the garden'?"
>
> And the woman said to the serpent, "We may eat the fruit of the trees of the garden; but of the fruit of the tree

which is in the midst of the garden, God has said, 'You shall not eat it, nor shall you touch it, lest you die.'"

Then the serpent said to the woman, "You will not surely die. For God knows that in the day you eat of it your eyes will be opened, and you will be like God, knowing good and evil."

So when the woman saw that the tree was good for food, that it was pleasant to the eyes, and a tree desirable to make one wise, she took of its fruit and ate. She also gave to her husband with her, and he ate.

Then the eyes of both of them were opened, and they knew that they were naked; and they sewed fig leaves together and made themselves coverings. (Genesis 3:1–7)

Let's consider the way we so often fall prey to the tempter based on the same weakness our mother Eve displayed. Something looks good, and the man in our life isn't coming through to provide it for us. Or to protect us from it, as in the case of Eve's husband. (Notice that God's Word mentions Adam was with her and that he ate at her offering.) The clever words of the serpent and the beautiful, succulent fruit of the tree created a powerful catalyst for Eve to take matters into her own hands. She bought into the lie, even as she bit into the bittersweet fruit of her own false power.

You and I must acknowledge that wanting to take matters into our own hands can be an easy excuse for pulling our own fruit off the tree. Sometimes we do it because a situation is intolerable and we see no other way out. But, in many cases, we simply react out of fear and insecurity and seize power at any opportunity—often as we saw our own mothers do. We have no faith in the relationship and our place in it. We do not trust. And if our relationships with men are not built on trust to begin with, when the serpents come along—and they always do—we will be tempted to take control instead of acting as a partner and trusting our husband's leadership.

Whether we watched our mothers become Eves and manipulate power in their relationships with men or whether we gravitate toward this in our own fearful desire to protect ourselves, we must reconsider and repent of any attempt to control the men in our lives. Of course, we lack the power to do this all by ourselves—even if we did have a good role model in our mother. That's why we must seek our Lord's love and the divine power of the Holy Spirit to love and give beyond ourselves. If you know you struggle with manipulating the men in your life, I encourage you to reflect on the following Scripture. It's the antidote to the swill of poison the serpents in our lives often peddle:

> Love suffers long and is kind; love does not envy; love does not parade itself, is not puffed up; does not behave rudely, does not seek its own, is not provoked, thinks no evil; does not rejoice in iniquity, but rejoices in the truth; bears all things, believes all things, hopes all things, endures all things. Love never fails. (1 Corinthians 13:4–8)

This kind of love never needs to manipulate to feel its own worth. This kind of love is from our Lord and kindles a fire in our hearts for those we love that transcends our circumstances. It's the foundation for standing on our own, knowing our true worth, and being open to the love of godly men in our lives.

Perhaps, dear lady, you can spend some time in prayer and reflect on ways you are tempted to pick forbidden fruit in your own life's relationships. Consider using the following prayer as a model to get you started:

———————————— ✐ ————————————

Dear God, You are the Keeper of my heart. Please help me to see the ways in which I manipulate and seek to control my relationships instead of trusting You. Allow me to rest in You and my confidence as Your beautiful child. Allow me to risk my heart at the right times with the right man. Enable me to see the ways I may have absorbed my mother's fears and repeated her strategies with men. Give me insight into my parents' relationship so I can learn and grow from the best parts of their love. Help me to love the way You love, to see the way You see. Amen.

———————————— ✐ ————————————

A Mother's Heart

As we've explored in this chapter, there are certainly many lessons we learned from our mothers, both about our identities as women and about our relationships to men. While some of these lessons may reflect our mothers' issues and personal baggage, so much of what our mothers gave us must be celebrated. The strength and compassion, the resilience and tenderness, the ability to risk loving and to persevere in our pursuit of God's best for us. As I've gotten older, started my own home with my husband, and raised our children, I've appreciated my mother in richer and deeper ways. The sacrifices she made that I often took for granted while growing up. The personal struggles she pushed through to raise her children after the loss of her husband. Her faith in God's goodness even in the midst of painful circumstances. Her quiet affirmation of my special, feminine soul. In so many ways, she taught me to know my worth, to seek out beauty throughout my life's journey, and to be the lady that our Lord created me to be. I am so humbled and grateful for the gifts she has given me and her legacy that I can continue to pass on to my children and their children some day.

Yes, we may have some aspects of our relationship with our mothers we wish were different. However, we must not let those issues blind us to the wonderful parts of our heart's foundation that she helped build in us. We must use these lessons as the scaffolding of our own legacy that we wish to leave to those around us: our family and friends, our children and grandchildren.

No matter how they might have failed us, our mothers planted seeds of joy and hope in us simply by giving us the gift of life. From these tender buds, we can allow the garden of our souls to blossom and bring grace and beauty to those around us. I believe this is part of our unique calling as women—part of the special gift we can bring to the men in our lives: the ability to display a mother's heart. We may not have birth children of our own but we can love others unconditionally as our Creator loves us. We don't need to baby the special man in our lives (well, sometimes!) in order to remind him of the soul nourishment that a feminine perspective can bring.

So, dear sister, give thanks for the mother whom God used to bring you into this world. Be grateful for the village mothers who have nurtured and modeled their love of you. And carry on their tradition of revealing God's grace in the lives of those around you. Be blessed in the sisterhood of who you are as a unique woman of God!

———————— ⟶ ————————

Dear Lord, I give You thanks and praise for the wonderful gift of mothers in my life. Please allow me to draw on those best parts of my mother's life and use her legacy to further my journey as Your daughter. As I relate to other men, I ask that I would display the uniqueness of what it means to be feminine. Please help me to shine with Your beauty, grace, and truth into the lives of those around me. May I inspire and nurture other girls and women and may I bless the men with whom I relate. Amen.

———————— ⟶ ————————

Questions and Suggestions

1. Who were your maternal role models while you were growing up? What did you learn about femininity and being female from these women?

2. How would you describe your relationship with your mother when you were a girl? How would you describe it now?

3. Make a list of all the messages you learned from Mama about what it means to be a woman and to carry out her responsibilites. Include items on personal appearance, housekeeping, cooking, dating, and child-rearing.

4. Watch a film that explores mother-daughter relationships and then write a journal entry on how it makes you feel. You might consider watching *Steel Magnolias*, *Terms of Endearment*, *The Color Purple*, or *Pride and Prejudice*.

5. What did you learn about how women relate to men based on your mom and other role models? Try to describe the way your mother related to your father and other important men in her life.

6. How are the ways you relate to men similar to what you learned and observed from your mother?

7. Write a letter to your mother describing your current struggles and uncertainties regarding how you feel about yourself as a woman and how you relate to the important men in your life. Prayerfully consider whether you keep the letter for yourself or send it to her.

4

Bad Boys and Good Men:
Extreme Attractions

Have you ever seen one of those desktop toys that executives keep in their offices? It's a row of metal balls, like giant ball bearings, lined up and suspended by wires. Someone gave one of these gadgets to my husband, and our youngest son loves to play with it whenever he visits his daddy's office. When you pull back the ball on one end and drop it back down to clack against its neighbor, the resulting reverberations make the ball on the other end jump out. It then returns and makes the original ball jump out. And so forth, like a pendulum. I recall something from my school science classes about Newton's law of reactions: For every action there is an equal and opposite reaction.

I mention this toy, and Newton's law, because of the way, I believe, it symbolizes the dynamic between a woman's parents and the men she finds attractive. You may have noticed that in the preceding two chapters I didn't address one of the most direct ways our fathers and mothers influence our relationships with the opposite sex: in our attraction to certain kinds of men. Most of us would agree that our relationship with our parents has a strong bearing on the kind of men to whom we're attracted. So often women are looking to find in their boyfriend the affirmation, approval, and affection they didn't receive from Daddy. Or they may be trying to gain Mama's approval or prove her wrong by their choice of men. In some cases, the man to whom they're attracted may even resemble their father—his mannerisms, speech, the way he dresses. On the other hand, a father's attributes may be the last thing women want to see when they look into the eyes of the men who melt their hearts. Often it does seem the dynamic is one of extremes.

Does this ring true for you, sister? I encourage you to think about your own experiences and those of your friends. At the risk of overgeneralizing, it seems women (and we can include men in this "pendulum effect," too!) are either attracted to men very similar to their fathers or the total opposite. I'm aware that our relationships are much more complex than this, but I do find it helpful to be aware of what you're looking for in a man and see how that might have roots in your upbringing. Allow me to share one of my own discoveries of this insight as we continue to examine the pendulum effect.

Rebel with a Cause

When my oldest daughter was a young teenager, I watched her go through one of her very first crushes on a boy I'll call Jimmy. He was a couple of years older than she and had muscular shoulders and brooding, deep-set eyes. He wore "cool clothes," baggy jeans and a Starter jacket, crooked ball cap and a thick gold chain. He had his own souped-up car. According to my daughter, his smile could light up an entire room, but when she finally introduced him to me after a school ball game, I wasn't that impressed.

A few weeks later when Jimmy asked her out, I certainly had my reservations. I didn't forbid my daughter from going out with him, but I told her I'd prefer she didn't. Stick to a group of friends going out together, I told her.

"What is it about Jimmy that you don't like?" she asked. "Why don't you want me to go out with him?"

She was forcing me to try to put my finger on it. "I hate to sound old-fashioned," I started, "but Jimmy hasn't convinced me that he's as cool and in control as he wants you to think. He wants to be a rebel, but he hasn't found his cause yet."

"What does that mean?" she asked. "You think he's trouble just because he dresses hipper and acts cooler than the other boys we know?"

"Not necessarily trouble," I said. "He's just not what he appears to be. He hasn't found himself yet."

Despite my wishful thinking, my daughter continued to hang around Jimmy. I kept close tabs on her involvement with him and became a bit concerned when she stopped telling me much about him and their time together. Was she seeing him just to spite me? Was there more to this young man than I was allowing?

I quickly discovered my original hunch was right on target. After several weeks went by, my daughter sheepishly admitted that Jimmy really wasn't different from any of the other boys she knew. Beneath his steely gaze and hip-hop persona, he was just as unsure of himself, just as silly, just as moody as her brothers and other male peers. She told me, "I still like him, but we're just friends." Her infatuation had burst like a soap bubble in the wind. But that's not the end of the story.

A few more weeks went by, and I noticed that she was still seeing Jimmy. When I inquired if she'd changed her mind again (a teenager's prerogative), she told me that no, they were still just friends. "But I have discovered something," she confessed. "The more I hang out with Jimmy, the more other people protest and try to warn me about how bad he is. Jimmy has them fooled with his image, just like he'd impressed me at first, and so they assume the worst and want to protect me." She looked up at me and concluded, "It's funny, but this made me want to continue going out with him all the more, even though he and I were only friends. What's up with that?"

My daughter and I proceeded to have a thoughtful conversation about Jimmy's appeal and what she was gaining by being associated with him. The appeal, as best I can discern from thinking through my daughter's words and my own experience, is that Jimmy appeared tough, mature, and in control. He seemed to possess the currency required to move about in the adult economy, even while he clearly didn't buy into the well-behaved conformity that we adults want from teens.

My daughter wanted the same kind of "money" in her identity bank. This combination is a powerful convergence for a teenage female on the brink between girlhood and womanhood. Part of her so longed to be an adult, a grown-up. To possess the poise and beauty of the adult women she observed, along with the grace and wisdom of her role models. Part of her wanted to remain a little girl, just having fun and needing the security of her family. One moment she was playing dress-up with her girlfriends from elementary school; the next she wanted to wear lipstick and have young men take notice. Adolescence is such a crazy time! (I remember it too well.) Bodies mature faster than a mind can keep up emotionally or socially. My daughter wanted the best of both worlds: the security and innocence of being a little girl, and the privileges and glamour of being a woman. Out of these conflicting emotions, she was searching for someone to help her cross over to full adulthood. Jimmy appeared to have made the leap into manhood without the stodgy wardrobe and overly responsible attitude of most grown-ups she knew. He seemed exciting and a bit dangerous—free from the limitations of childhood and yet resistant to the obligations of adulthood.

As you may have guessed, dear sister, the key words here are "appeared" and "seemed." In preparing to write about this, I asked my daughter to read over the last few paragraphs. She laughed and said, "Yeah, Jimmy and I are still friends, but he's such a goof. I discovered that Jimmy was much more like me than anyone would ever have guessed: unsure of himself, awkward, afraid, a kid just wishin' his way into adulthood. His cultivated image worked on most people—they all spoke of him as if he were a hardened ex-con rather than a sixteen-year-old boy! I guess I wanted to have others perceive me as just as grown up, just as tough and cool and sure of myself."

Perhaps you can recall an experience similar to this from your days in junior or high school. Maybe you had your own Jimmy who helped you change your image or make the jump from the way your family and friends viewed you as a girl. Maybe you've experienced a similar experience with your own daughter or granddaughter. All of us most likely had the same basic reason for our attraction to "bad boys": We simply wanted the attention of a young man who was different, who stood out as being clearly on the other side of manhood. We were attracted to and searching for this kind of man. Someone who made us feel grown up and rebellious at the same time—someone of whom others didn't approve. But while what we experienced in adolescence may factor into how we feel about men like this, I believe that if we are still attracted to them by the time we're adult women, there are some other issues going on.

Opposites Attract

"She's got *issues*," my girlfriend said, pointing out the erratic behavior of another of our friends. "Why else would she stay with that no-good boyfriend of hers?" Why, indeed, we may ask. Most of us can think of a friend or family member who always seems to be attracted to the "wrong type."

And it seems so crystal clear to us from the outside looking in: attractive, smart, educated women destined to remain forever attracted to the wrong kind of men—dangerous, lazy, ambitionless men who drain the energy out of their ladies like leeches. You probably have a relative or girlfriend right now who's in a relationship with a man you and the rest of her friends deem a "loser." While you want to give such a man the benefit of the doubt and you try to remember he's a real person, not just a label, he often seems determined to prove you wrong.

You may recall such a relationship you yourself had in the past. More important, deep down you may know you're in that kind of relationship right now.

So why is it so hard to break out of these relationships? What's the appeal in them? I believe the answers to these two questions fall into a couple of main categories: identification and reformation. Let's consider identity-based attractions first.

Magnetic Attractions. If we think of ourselves and the bad boy to whom we're attracted as magnets, then this first category often finds us attracted like opposite magnetic poles. There's a strong pull based on the way he looks, the image he has, the way he behaves, the way he's different than everyone else. In this identification dynamic, we're still looking for ourselves, still unsure of who we want to be, and his confidence and authority seem irresistible. Many times he appears to be our opposite: the old cliché about bad boys attracting good girls. Like my daughter's attraction to Jimmy, the pull is more about wanting to be empowered—to be an adult woman—than about wanting to be "bad" ourselves. It's as if we're trying to line up and identify our own magnet's north pole and south pole based on our pull to him.

I believe this is a core part of what we're looking for: fulfillment. For our desire to be named and identified. Please don't think I'm too old-fashioned; it's not that we must have a man to know who we are. But often we look for ourselves in those we find attractive. If our parents aren't helping us discover our identities, then we look to other relationships. We look to the man. Like Adam recognizing Eve as part of himself in the Garden and naming her, we want to be seen and known and appreciated for who we are.

> And the LORD God caused a deep sleep to fall on Adam, and he slept; and He took one of his ribs, and closed up the flesh in its place.
> Then the rib which the LORD God had taken from man He made into a woman, and He brought her to the man.
> And Adam said:
> "This is now bone of my bones
> And flesh of my flesh;
> She shall be called Woman,
> Because she was taken out of Man." (Genesis 2:21–23)

Often the bad boy is also someone seeking his own identity. He feels that he doesn't belong, doesn't fit in with his buddies on their sports teams or with their attitudes. He likely didn't have a father who served as a positive role model. So he becomes intent on creating his own unique and separate identity as someone who's tough, who is to be feared, who commands respect.

The problem with this kind of attraction, however, is that rarely do the individuals allow themselves to move beyond the roles they're playing. Ironically enough, he doesn't know who he is and hopes his woman can help name him. She doesn't know who she is and hopes her man can help name her. It's like two amnesia victims trying to tell each other who they are!

Without a sense of our own identity, our own special worth and value apart from any relationship we enter into, we will likely be frustrated and left unsatisfied. Ideally, our identity as an individual is something we should receive from our parents, especially from our father or village father. And ultimately it's something we must find in our relationship with our heavenly Father—our identity as the King's daughter and our value as His precious child. As much as we want to be known and named by our man—a legitimate longing, I believe—we must first know who we are in the presence of our Lord.

If this is an area of struggle for you, please consider the following prayer as a way of expressing your heart's desire.

Dear heavenly Father, You know how much I long to know who I truly am. Please allow me a deep awareness of what it means for me to be Your child, Your precious daughter, the apple of Your eye. Help me not to place my identity outside myself, looking for it in the men who are seeking it themselves. Give me the confidence of Your promises and the ability to love myself as You love me. Amen.

The Ultimate Makeover. The second category is *reformation,* or the "ultimate makeover," as one friend described her attempts to change her bad boy. This attraction often flows out of our sincere intention to be a positive influence on our man. We know his imperfections but see beyond his tough appearance into a soft heart. We believe that if we only love and help him, he'll change his behaviors, lose his addictions, and become a model citizen. We can see how special and sensitive our man is beneath his appearance as a tough guy or bully. And we want everyone else to see it, too. We want our bad boy to reform his ways and be tamed into domestic husband material. Instead of trying to label our own magnet based on the attraction of his magnet, we try to change the direction of his pull altogether. It's as if we want to make his north pole the south pole and vice versa. And it's like trying to take a fierce rottweiler and turn it into a toy poodle.

Once again, let me make a disclaimer. As you will see in the following chapters, I believe it's vitally important for a woman to love and believe in her man. She can provide him with heart support and deep soul encouragement at levels no one else in his life can touch. I believe this is part of a wife's calling—to become one with her husband. Her unconditional love and support can indeed change his life and help him become more of who God wants him to be. However, no one can change another person unless he wants to change himself. Too often in this kind of relationship, the bad boy doesn't want to change. He may just want the best of both worlds: doing what he wants without considering consequences while soaking up the makeover attention from his woman. This man isn't going to change just because an optimistic woman wants him to change.

Why would a woman continue to be attracted to a man who refuses to change his ways, who continues to hurt her and neglect their relationship? From what I've seen, these women are often tenderhearted, compassionate, and oblivious to their own needs. They are far too often the rescuers and enablers in their families, believing that if they can only get their act together, their parents or siblings will stop fighting, quit drinking, end the abuse, and live happily ever after. Others may simply be tender- hearted women of deep empathy and compassion who always want to give their men the benefit of the doubt. Regardless, these women carry this into their relationships with men and believe they can change them like renovating an old house.

I recall a lovely older woman who approached me one Sun- day after church and asked to speak with me. By her heavy tone and tear-streaked face, I knew she was really hurting. We ducked into an empty classroom and she poured her heart out to me.

"I keep praying for my man, Sister Jakes," she started. "But the Lord don't seem to be answering my prayers."

I nodded and offered her a tissue. She continued: "Every weekend he drinks and stays out late with his buddies. He says things he don't mean when he drinks too much. He spends all his money on liquor and gambling and then can't help me pay the bills. He won't come to church with me. And I'm so afraid that something's gonna happen to him before he knows the Lord. I keep praying and praying, but he don't change."

Comforting her as best I could, I offered the words the Spirit laid on my heart. "You can only change yourself, my dear sister. He will never change until he wants to. No matter how badly you want it for him, if he doesn't want to change, then he's going to keep on doing what he's doing. If fact, maybe you should let him face some of the consequences of his own actions."

"What do you mean, sister?" she asked.

"You say that he doesn't help you with the bills because he

spends his money on liquor and gambling. So maybe you don't give him your hard-earned money when he comes begging for it. Maybe you let him see what it's like with no food in the house or with the power turned off. I mean no disrespect, but it sounds like you're taking mighty good care of him. There's no reason for him to change as long as you're there to mama him. Keep praying for him, but let him find out what he's doing to himself."

I was afraid I'd said far too much but felt peace about the words God laid on my heart. The woman looked angrily at me at first, as if I didn't understand, and then she started crying. We prayed together and set up a time to meet again later in the week. By the time we next spoke, she was beginning to realize she could not change her man, even as badly as she wanted to.

This sounds like such a harsh reality. But the truth remains that only our God can change a man's heart—if that man is willing to be changed and opened up from the inside out by the power of the Spirit. It's hard to realize that one's own power is limited, that it's not within our control to change the situation, but that is the hard truth. It's not that we don't have influence on those we love, and it's not that our love doesn't make a powerful difference in our man's life. It's simply that his heart must want the same thing as our heart, and that we both are seeking God's heart in your relationship.

I encourage you, dear reader, to seek the Lord's wisdom as you discern whether or not you're trying to change a man who doesn't want to be changed. The following prayer might give words to some of your heart's struggles.

Dear Lord, You know how much I love this man in my life. You know how hard I've tried to help him know You, how much I've wanted him

*to change. But I confess that I can't change him; only you can change a
man's heart. I pray for him now that You would do a mighty work and
reveal Your goodness to him. I let go of trying to make him someone he's
not, and I entrust him to You. Help me to know how best to love You
and love myself. Amen.*

———————————— ∽ ————————————

A Few Good Men

If a woman's attractions to a so-called bad boy are surrounded by
more complex issues, such as those of identity or the desire to reform him, how does she move on? How does she begin to tell the
difference between a bad boy and a good man?

I believe the primary factors in this distinction are twofold: his
maturity level and his willingness to persevere. Let's first consider what I mean by maturity because it certainly encompasses
more than just physical growth. We've all known fresh-faced
teenagers who, through the fires of life circumstances, were
forged into men. And we've known grizzled forty-year-olds who
remained childlike in their self-absorption and need for toys.
Maturity is much more than just chronological age. It has to do
with a man's emotional stability, his perspective on life, and his
relationship with God. These are the factors that separate the
men from the boys. A mature man is willing to strive for more
and welcomes feedback from the woman in his life. He has a vision for himself, often one given to him by an older man (his own
father or mentor perhaps), that goes beyond where he is in the
present. A mature man is capable of loving and sacrificing for the
woman in his life and for his God-given goals. He can see the big
picture and not just respond to the feel-good gratification of the

day. He wants to leave a legacy in all that he does, for his family and for the glory of God.

The other distinction here between "bad" and "good"—perseverance—refers to not just the way we might evaluate a man's behavior according to biblical categories. It's easy enough to say that taking drugs or cheating on one's spouse is wrong and that staying sober and remaining faithful is right. But here's where I'm afraid many of us get confused about what a good man really is. As we begin making the distinction between boys and men, we may realize we're expecting too much. Perhaps we women who hope to reform our men are especially prone to this. The notion of a *good* man becomes the *ideal* man, the perfect man, the man who never lets us down. We may know this isn't true in our minds, but our hearts clings to this stubborn and subtle belief that if our man is truly a good man, he'll do everything right.

That's not the case, of course. We're all human, all flawed and imperfect, all struggling to be better men and women by the grace of God. Would you like being held to a standard of perfection? Most of us want to be loved unconditionally, even as we maintain the trust we've worked hard to earn and maintain. Similarly, a good man is not without flaws and failures. No, a good man is simply one who gets back on his feet after he falls, who keeps persevering after righteousness because of his hope and trust in the Lord.

Sister, I believe this is how you give your heart to a man: by believing that despite his failures and weaknesses, he's committed to loving God and loving you. Consider many of the men we see in the Bible, from Adam (why didn't he speak up and protect Eve from the serpent's crafty words?) to Abraham (talk about a man who made some mistakes—like attempting to pass off his wife as his sister!) to Jacob (caught up with two sisters—could be the first soap-opera love triangle ever recorded!). Or better yet, someone like David, described as a "man after God's own heart." No matter how many huge mistakes he made—and he made some whoppers (lusting after Bathsheba, committing adultery with her, having her husband killed, just to name a few)—he never gave up on himself or God's ability to forgive and redeem him.

Read his words from Psalm 51:

> Have mercy upon me, O God,
> According to Your lovingkindness;
> According to the multitude of Your tender mercies,
> Blot out my transgressions.
> Wash me thoroughly from my iniquity,
> And cleanse me from my sin . . .
> Create in me a clean heart, O God,
> And renew a steadfast spirit within me.
> Do not cast me away from Your presence,
> And do not take Your Holy Spirit from me.
> Restore to me the joy of Your salvation,
> And uphold me by Your generous Spirit.
> Then I will teach transgressors Your ways,
> And sinners shall be converted to You. (vv. 1–2, 10–13)

Certainly this is a prayer for all of us as we strive to embrace the Lord's mercy and goodness and move on from our mistakes and failures. This is the kind of man I believe we can call "good." One who is mature enough to know he needs to depend on the Lord and who is committed to persevering through the storms of life. This is the kind of man worth waiting for.

Having said that, a good man comes in many different shapes and sizes. He may even look like a bad boy on the outside, but through his words, behavior, and attitude he demonstrates the maturity and perseverance of a good man. And this is where we must consider our heart's ability to forgive when he fails and begin the process of trusting and loving in a new chapter of the relationship. With such forgiveness and perseverance in mind, is there a time when you should end your relationship with a bad boy? Should you quit hoping that he'll become a good man?

This is a question that comes up with many of the ladies I counsel. "Should I stay with him?" they ask me. "He says he's going to change." Without knowing your specific situation, this is such a difficult question to answer. We know that we serve a God of the impossible who can change men's hearts and transform their lives. Is there evidence of God's presence in your man even as he stumbles occasionally? Is his desire to change sincere? If you love him and see him genuinely working to change old habits or mistakes, don't be afraid to risk your heart again and stick out the relationship's rocky patches.

On the other hand, don't be fooled by slick words that have no actions to back them up. Generally speaking, most bad boys know how to say what you want to hear. They can promise you the moon and the sun, but if they are not actively pursuing the Lord and His changes in their life, you must be willing to move on. It sounds harsh, perhaps, because you want to give them the benefit of the doubt and to know that God can change them. And He can. But you must remember that your man must be willing to allow God to change him.

I know real life and relationships are more complicated than this. It's easy for me to say you should leave behind you the bad boys who aren't willing to change. I realize that you may have a history together, children together, and the embers of a once-powerful passion. But I also know you must "get real" with yourself at some point; you must seek the Lord's wisdom in prayer and realize you cannot change him, no matter how hard you try. Look for fruit in his life that he wants to change before sticking it out too much longer.

Perhaps you've never been attracted to "bad boys." Nonetheless, I think we all know what it is to long for a good man. As you prepare to move on and consider how to wait patiently for the man God may bring for you, I encourage you to think about the kind of man you long for in your life. Whether you've been married for decades or whether you're young, single, and not particularly interested in a man right now, I think you need to know what you're looking for, either in the husband who already shares your life, or in the man you may meet this very day. Not a perfect man, but a good man. With such a target in mind, let's move forward and see what happens as you approach the bull's-eye.

———————————— ✑ ————————————

Dear Creator, I give You thanks for the various men in my life so far. I praise You for the good men who have modeled Your character and love to me. I pray these would be the men to whom I am most attracted. I thank You as well for the so-called "bad boys" and ask that I would learn what You have to teach me through my interactions with them. Please allow me to see Your handiwork in the lives of good men as well as the bad boys who may be resisting Your presence in their lives. Help me to know my boundaries, when to guard my heart, and when to risk vulnerability. Give me patience as I wait and gratitude when I find the man You may send into my life. Amen.

———————————— ✑ ————————————

Questions and Suggestions

1. How would you define or describe a "bad boy"? What do you believe motivates these men's "bad" image and lifestyle?

2. Whether you've ever been in a relationship with one or not, what attracts you to a bad boy? What's not so attractive about him?

3. Watch your favorite "bad boy" movie and make a list of defining characteristics of the film's hero-rebel. Go over your list and consider which traits you find attractive and which ones turn you off.

4. If you've struggled in being attracted to bad boys more than you'd like, try to investigate the relationship between this attraction and the messages you picked up from your parents. If you find you're reacting to their messages, consider ways to pursue a good man. You might purchase one of those desktop pendulums as a reminder not to react to the extremes.

5. Do you agree that women often are attracted to men as a result of their extreme reaction to their parents' messages about relationship? Why or why not?

6. In your journal write out a classified-ad description of a "good man." What are the essential traits you want him to have? Who are the older male role models who embody these traits in your circle?

PART 2

I Stand Before Him:
Seeing Yourself
in His Eyes

5

Single but Not Satisfied:
Waiting Without Despair

It's a clear, starlit night. By moonlight a beautiful woman is gently led by a handsome man through a lush grove of trees. They pause beneath a giant oak, silhouetted on the horizon. Suddenly, all its branches flare up like an oversized Christmas tree with hundreds of twinkling lights. The man pulls out a velvet box. Inside, a stunning diamond—every bit as big as one of the lights on the tree—jumps out at the speechless woman. Will she marry him? Of course she will! The violin music plays, they kiss to seal the engagement, and . . . the jewelry store's next sale flashes across the screen.

Have you seen an advertisement like this? How did it make you feel? In the last chapter we looked at some of our attractions to bad boys—to men we know are wrong for us. While these attractions can be and are often affected by our parents, they also are reinforced by our culture and the media as they are filtered through our own sense of loneliness. So much of what we see, hear, and experience is geared to manipulate our emotions and make us feel conspicuous if we're single or alone.

Much has been made of the notion that if a woman isn't married by age thirty, she has as great a chance of being struck by lightning or winning the lottery as marrying her man. Similarly, many movies portray unlikely attractions between Ken- and Barbie-looking actors that typically yield comedic results and passionate romance. Television shows, from sitcoms to reality programs, focus on dating, breakups, reunions, and fairy-tale endings. On the small screen, attractive bachelors and bachelorettes have multiple partners from which to choose. No one has to be alone for long.

Repeatedly, the message seems to be that you're not okay unless some man is pursuing you or you're searching for him. And once you find him, well, your life should be lived happily ever after. You're told you need a man to be happy and romance is the be-all and end-all to living a happy life. Even if you know otherwise, our culture is so saturated with these messages that it's difficult to overcome their effect on us.

These kinds of cultural messages also support an over-emphasis on youth and beauty. Why are so many older women willing to visit the plastic surgeon? Why are so many women discontent with the looks God gave them? The equation seems to work something like this: In order to be desirable, you must be young and attractive; in order to look young(er!) and attractive, you must use a particular company's products. It's as if the glossy advertisements in the fashion magazines whisper, "You better hurry, ladies! Time's running out. If you don't attract a man now, it will be too late too soon. Buy this product and there might be hope for even you." In our consumer-driven society, the emphasis on appearance is usually pitched to make you feel insecure about yourself in front of the opposite sex. You need to use this shampoo, wear these shoes, smell like this fragrance, and dress like this model if you're going to have any shot at looking good enough to attract and keep a man.

Must you buy into this belief that new beauty products will lead us to your heart's desire? What happens if you spend all that money, look better than you have a right to, and are still alone? Then what? What does it mean to be single today?

Alone in a Crowd

So many of the single ladies who seek me for counsel have struggles with their solitary state. The aloneness, the feeling of being different from everyone else. The feeling that everyone else around you is part of a couple or ahead of you in this pursuit of passion and purpose with a man. Perhaps this is your greatest struggle as well. And many of the ladies with whom I speak tell me it's not that they're pining away like an old maid in a tearjerker movie. They've been in relationships before, have sometimes been married before, but it just hasn't worked out. They feel something must be wrong with them. The peer pressure mounts and our culture continues to elevate romance as the epitome of all life has to offer.

One of my friends calls this her chronic battle with the "single virus." She desperately wants a cure and will temporarily think she's found one in her latest boyfriend. But six months later they've broken up and she's again by herself, alone in a crowd. In response to her request for my advice about how to meet her soul mate, I shared two significant truths I think apply to many ladies suffering this same affliction. First, when you find yourself in a season of singleness, you must not compromise what you're looking for. And second, dear reader, while you're looking and waiting on the

Lord to provide the right man in your life, you must not compromise yourself.

Compromise in the First Degree. The first kind of compromise often perpetuates the same frustrations and relational patterns over and over again. Perhaps you find yourself attracted to your ideal man, only he's always unavailable because he's a married man. Or you find yourself attracted to the bad boys because of their charisma and flash and charm. You want to walk alongside a strong, tender gentleman who has purpose in his step and a twinkle in his eye, but you find yourself constantly tripping behind the heels of a smooth-talking charmer who's not sure where he wants to go or how to get there. What you truly long for is stability and commitment and someone who shares your faith and other life values.

As painful as it may be in the short term, you must be realistic enough to break the pattern and set your sights on a partner for life. In other words, dear sister, at some point you're going to have to stop shopping for vegetables in the candy store! Not that you can't meet a wonderful, stable, Christian man in the nightclub or singles bar, but the odds are much greater that you'll meet someone who simply wants to have a no-strings-attached good time. On the other hand, you may be "shopping" in the right places—the gym, church, or a book group—but still haven't found the right man at the right time. In either case, you must focus on what you truly desire in a life partner. Not perfection, mind you, because you're not perfect either, but the qualities that matter most to you, such as his faith and walk before the Lord, his honesty and integrity, his compassion and sense of humor, his perseverance and playfulness. It's not that I encourage you to use this as a checklist, but simply as a standard to help remind yourself of your true heart's desire.

Second-Degree Burns. The second tendency to compromise often goes hand in hand with the first. Since ladies in single seasons of life often struggle with such loneliness and low self-esteem, they sometimes become willing to compromise their hearts and their bodies in attempts to mask the symptoms or alleviate their pain. This may take the form of sporadic one-night stands or late nights on the phone chat line pretending intimacy with total strangers. It may appear as bingeing on ice cream and pound cake or nonstop shopping on-line. Most ladies know this is not good for them and experience a deep shame that may only compound their self-conscious awareness of being single. They long to remain pure and wholesome, but the pain of being single simply seems too much to bear at times. They know they need help but don't know how to break the addictive cycle of numbing their pain.

I recall a conversation with a lady my age who led a Bible study we had been in for several years. Trim and immaculately dressed, she was someone I admired and respected because of her warmth as well as her discipline. While she had been single her entire life, she never seemed to stress about it. "God will bring the right man at the right time," she'd say quietly whenever the topic came up. In the meantime, she had gotten on with her life by completing a graduate degree in business and starting her own consulting firm. She often traveled and seemed to keep herself too busy to focus on her single status. Then one weekend I received a call from her.

"Serita," she whispered, "I'm going out of town on business Monday and really need your prayers." I asked her how I could pray, and she began crying and asked to meet me in person. We set up an appointment for coffee the next day, and then she poured her heart out to me.

"Whenever I travel, I . . . I pick up men in the hotel bar," she said tearfully. "At first it was exciting and even fun—a kind of game. But it's gotten to where I do it almost automatically. Whenever I feel lonely or afraid, I simply start looking at my next business trip and planning when I can pick someone up. I feel so ashamed and dirty. I know I'm never going to meet the right man at the right time if I keep looking in the wrong places."

I listened and thanked her for the privilege of her trust. As we prepared to pray together, I reminded her of God's promises to forgive us and give us His grace through the gift of His Son Jesus: "If we confess our sins, He is faithful and just to forgive us our sins and to cleanse us from all unrighteousness" (1 John 1:9). I have continued to pray for this dear, courageous sister who was no longer willing to compromise herself. It struck me as ironic that the very issue that drove her to compromise herself in the first place—the pain of her aloneness—also compounded and hid her attempts at numbing that same pain. In other words, because she's single, there was no one in her life to help her combat the temptations in her life. That's why it was so good and important for her to talk to someone, to break the silence of her shameful secret. She was then able to get back on her feet, picked up and dusted off by her heavenly Father, so she could stand tall and continue on her journey once more.

I believe such confession and community are the most powerful ways to combat this tendency to compromise one in the midst of a painful single season. If you struggle in this area, I encourage you to seek out other trustworthy women and un-burden your heart. Ask them to hold you accountable and to pray for you. Call them when you need to stare down the enemy to keep yourself pure for the man upon whom you wait. The other crucial way to combat the enemy in this battle is to keep the communication lines wide open between you and the Lord. In pursuit of His loving mercy and protection, you might find the following prayer helpful in voicing some of your concerns.

Dear Keeper of my Soul, I come before You now knowing that You see my heart and know all my secrets. Please forgive me, Father, for those times I've settled for less than Your best, for those times I've been impatient and tried to take matters into my own hands. I confess that I sometimes compromise my standards, and Yours, amid the pain and frustration I experience in my loneliness. Protect me from the snares of the enemy. Restore my heart and cleanse me of all unrighteousness. Help me to know Your love for me and allow You to nourish and sustain me, even while keeping the desires of my heart alive. Please send Your man in Your time, and give me patience and trust in You along the way. Amen.

Single State of Mind

Perhaps you don't struggle so much with compromising your standards or being tempted to numb the pain in your heart with unrighteous outlets. But the central question remains to nag at your soul: Why is it so hard to be single? How can you enjoy your life to the fullest without making it conditional around romance and a leading man in your life? In response to these questions, two important truths come to mind—one that you've likely heard before and one that may fly in the face of what you've heard before.

The first truth is that a woman must be *honest* about what she longs for and realize that only God can fulfill her soul. If you haven't been honest about this spiritual need, or you have it confused with your emotional and physical needs, it will be hard for you to have a healthy relationship with a man. In fact, if you haven't discovered your identity as God's child, being single remains a state of mind. So many women feel alone and incomplete, even in their marriages and relationships. They still feel single, no matter how many lovers and husbands they may have had. Like a moon without a planet around which to fix its orbit, these women scramble to find men at any cost. Something empty gnaws inside them and keeps them searching, looking for something to touch that deep hole in their heart.

Understand this: Your heart's fulfillment first comes from your relationship with the Lord. If you don't have that deep knowledge in your heart of His love for you, it doesn't matter how many perfect men come along and sweep you off your feet. In fact, you may know someone who has gone through several marriages or relationships with good men but continues to search. She thinks the right man should be able to fulfill her deepest needs and complete her in a way that will never leave her lacking. She wants a man to fulfill the spiritual thirst only God can quench.

Indeed, my sister, this kind of thirst emerges quite clearly in the story of Jesus' encounter with the Samaritan woman at the well. She has sought to fill the void within through her relationships with men. Notice how this woman responds to the Savior's invitation:

> A woman of Samaria came to draw water. Jesus said to her, "Give Me a drink." For His disciples had gone away into the city to buy food.
>
> Then the woman of Samaria said to Him, "How is it that You, being a Jew, ask a drink from me, a Samaritan woman?" For Jews have no dealings with Samaritans.
>
> Jesus answered and said to her, "If you knew the gift of God, and who it is who says to you, 'Give Me a drink,' you would have asked Him, and He would have given you living water." (John 4:6–10)

Let's pause the story right here for a moment. Consider the incredible compassion and disregard for cultural prejudice Jesus shows here simply by speaking to this woman. Jews were taught and conditioned to hate Samaritans, to regard them as unclean and unfit even to serve a Jew. Samaritan women often were regarded with even more contempt by Jewish men. Jesus doesn't hesitate, though. He is not put off by the color of her skin, by what she's done in the past, whom she's slept with, and how many times she's failed. No, He cuts through the cultural biases and barriers and speaks to the heart of this woman. He asks something of her.

Notice that she uses some of the same defenses we use today: "Lord, who am I to do what You ask of me?" we say. Then we fill in the blank with whatever we think disqualifies us from His love: "I'm single. I'm of mixed ethnicity. I'm divorced. I'm a gossip. I'm an adulteress. I had a baby out of wedlock. I slept with a married man. I've been raped. I do drugs." Dear woman, how have you responded to Jesus' request?

He responds by telling the woman that if she knew Him, she would drink of His living water and no longer thirst. In other words, she would see past her own issues, fears, and failures and receive the grace, peace, and forgiveness in the cooling liquid of His love. Have you tasted this refreshing draft of living water? Have you allowed Jesus' stream of mercy to drench your droughts and deserts? I encourage you to think about areas of your life and heart that need the life-giving moisture of a healing encounter with the Savior.

Let's continue with their interaction and see what else we can learn:

> The woman said to Him, "Sir, You have nothing to draw with, and the well is deep. Where then do You get that living water? Are You greater than our father Jacob, who gave us the well, and drank from it himself, as well as his sons and his livestock?"
>
> Jesus answered and said to her, "Whoever drinks of this water will thirst again, but whoever drinks of the water that I shall give him will never thirst. But the water that I shall give him will become in him a fountain of water springing up into everlasting life."
>
> The woman said to Him, "Sir, give me this water, that I may not thirst, nor come here to draw."
>
> Jesus said to her, "Go, call your husband, and come here." The woman answered and said, "I have no husband." Jesus said to her, "You have well said, 'I have no husband,' for you have had five husbands, and the one whom you now have is not your husband; in that you spoke truly." (John 4:11–18)

Notice how Jesus directs the course of their conversation. It seems so obvious and yet so vitally important that He goes directly from describing His living water to inquiring about the woman's husband(s). And in this connection, one question stands out. Since Jesus clearly knows what she's been up to, why would He ask her to call her husband? Is He being cruel since He knows how many men she's been through? Surely that is not our sinless Lord's intention. No, it seems much more for her benefit. Will she be honest with Him about whether she has a husband? Will she be honest with herself about where she has been trying to find a drink of water? Is she willing to admit that these many men haven't even begun to quench the thirst in her soul?

She is a single woman, or at least views herself as one, for she tells Jesus, "I have no husband" (4:17). He corrects her: telling her she has had husbands and she is now with a man who is not her husband. In other words, her singleness is a state of mind rather than her marital status. She has had men in her life, and while we don't know what kind of men they were, it is true that none of them could quench her soul's thirst. Only an encounter with the living God can provide that cold, clean water that so deeply satisfies. Only after you have visited Jacob's well and shared your heart with the Master will you be ready to meet a man who complements your being.

This is a painful truth that many women are still in the process of learning. We so long to find our soul's water in another person. It's tempting sometimes to make our worth conditional upon a man's approval. If he affirms us and adores us, then we must be okay. But no man—not our father, not our lover, not our husband—can fulfill us the way our God can. No matter where you may be on your journey of faith, sister,

I encourage you to let His living waters soak deep down into your bones.

Content but Not Satisfied

Once you've tasted of His living water and know it as the source of your life, being single is no longer such a desperate season. You have an inner peace that gives you strength and courage to live your life fully as a princess of the King. But even knowing your true identity and tasting the Father's love will not necessarily take away your heart's desire for a mate.

So often single ladies—especially in the church—are told to be single and satisfied, as if there's something wrong with their desire for a mate, as if God's love should take away their needs. Many women come to me in tears because they feel something is wrong with them. One single young woman confided to me, "Sister, I know and love the Lord. I pray daily and take joy in serving Him. But my heart still longs to have a husband and a family. I try to be content, but I can't stop my heart from hoping for a husband someday. What's wrong with me?"

Please hear me when I repeat the same message I told this child: "Dear woman, there is nothing wrong with you. God made you to be in a relationship. It's more than okay that you're not satisfied with being single. It doesn't mean you don't love Him. Being content doesn't mean you have to be just satisfied. If that were the case, none of us could ever hope for anything more."

The tension is that you must embrace being single for its season (and yes, the season may last a lifetime for some) but not be satisfied in it if, in your heart, you long for a companion, a lover, a soul mate. This is what I meant by that second truth that perhaps flies in the face of what you've always been told. Be content in the present while hoping to meet your man in the near future. I believe such a desire is God-given and a reflection of His holy desire for relationship with us Himself. He created the abundant beauty of the Garden, with its plants and trees, beasts and birds, sea creatures and oceans, but the Creation wasn't complete until God made man in His image: "And the LORD God said, 'It is not good that man should be alone; I will make him a helper comparable to him'" (Genesis 2:18). Our Lord designed us for relationship with a partner, a complement, someone comparable to us.

While some people may be called to a life of singleness, even still they experience loneliness and may long for a mate. But too often, I'm afraid, Christians have encouraged single women to bear their burden of singleness in silence with little sympathy. Another sister told me the women in her church called her "man crazy" just because she shared her disappointment that she wasn't yet married. Understandably, she stopped sharing her true feelings with these women and wondered if something was wrong with herself.

You must be honest with yourself if your desire is to be in a healthy relationship with a good man. You shouldn't suppress this desire by pretending you're not lonely or so independent that you don't need a man. It's normal for a single woman to want to find a man who loves her and whom she can love.

The trick, of course, is not to make your life conditional on finding the right man in your own time. This requires a level of patient expectancy and sacred hope in the Lord's goodness to provide His man in His time. Believe me, I know how hard it is to wait. Even after I met my future husband, I wanted to know for sure he was the one, when he would propose, and how many children we'd have. Patience comes from that inner garden our Lord waters and cultivates with His sustenance. As we trust in our Father's goodness and provision, we can then get on with our lives even as we long for a husband.

Once you've allowed yourself to express your desire for a mate, then you must examine how you may be living conditionally, putting everything on hold until you meet that special someone. Too often the temptation is to make your life conditional on finding Mr. Right instead of keeping on the right track. Even as you acknowledge your longing and keep your eyes attuned to the horizon for the man God may send your way, you must move forward as an independent woman.

You must get on with your life, with becoming the woman our Lord has called you to be, even as you acknowledge your longing for someone with whom to share it. You must surrender any tendency to live conditionally. Or, as my husband would say, you must step out of the shadows of life and into the spotlight to become God's leading lady. For the current season of your life's stage, you may or may not have a leading man. It takes courage and perseverance, but you must be willing to pursue your other dreams even while waiting on this one to be fulfilled. If you want to start your own business, but you're afraid you'll get too tied up with it and miss Mr. Right, you need to forge ahead and trust that Mr. Right may be a customer you'll meet up ahead. If you want to go back to school and finish your degree, but you're afraid you'll miss the man God has for you because you're not at the church singles group or even at the bar, trust that he may be waiting on you in the class. He may be teaching the class for all you know!

Don't put your dreams on hold, my sister, in hopes of waiting by the phone for your man to find you. You must trust that in the active pursuit of your own personal calling, your paths will intersect according to God's timing. It's hard to trust in this way when it seems you should always be looking and hoping. But stay focused on becoming the strong, tender woman of God you're called to become and trust that you'll meet a strong, compassionate man of God along your journey.

Longing for Love

I believe the temptation to give in to despair is the enemy's favorite weapon against most single people. It's because we are created to love and be loved in the image of our Creator, and when we're disconnected from God's love, or disappointed by others, we are torn between giving up all together and trying to make something happen for ourselves. Both strategies often lead to despair, a hopeless feeling that love is a good idea that may be working for all those other couples out there but sure isn't working for you.

Allowed to grow unchecked, such despair can fester into cynicism, a bitterness that trusts no one and risks nothing because your heart has become afraid and angry as love hasn't come along. And the sad thing is that such an attitude often repels any potential men you may encounter. People can sense such cynicism and identify it in your words and behavior. You have given up on love even as you're furious at God for not coming through for you. The enemy of your soul delights in this powerful trap that distances you from God and from other people and disconnects you from your true calling and giftedness.

To avoid such burnout and hopelessness, you must consider ways to combat the enemy and stay focused on your current season of life and God's present provision. First, I encourage you to avoid the extremes, if you can. As one sister told me, "Some days I want to join a convent, and other days I want to join an on-line dating service!" Talk to other single women or male friends who are struggling with disappointment in their lives. Enjoy getting together with friends and serving others in the church to combat the loneliness that is often the enemy's fertile soil for seeds of despair.

Next, as we've discussed, you must avoid getting stuck in a single state of mind in which you need a man to make you complete and fulfill you spiritually. Look to the Lord first in all that you do and lean not on your own understanding, the Scripture tells us (see Proverbs 3:5). Seek opportunities to trust Him with the needs and desires of your heart.

Please remember that we are certainly to find our soul's deepest refreshment and our true Lover in our relationship with God. He knows and loves us above all others. But I believe that part of His love for us is manifested through our relationship with others, often through a husband. Why else would He describe the relationship between Christ and the church as one between a bridegroom and his beloved? It is a holy and honorable desire to love and be loved, to know and be known, to grow and change together as one. Don't let anyone talk you out of your heart's desire or shame you for feeling like a little princess waiting for her prince to awaken her heart with a kiss. As the Shulamite bride says in the Song of Solomon, "Let him kiss me with the kisses of his mouth—for your love is better than wine" (Song of Solomon 1:2).

Finally, pamper yourself as you wait faithfully on the Lord's timing. By this I don't mean you should spoil yourself in a self-absorbed kind of way. Instead, I simply mean that while you struggle with your singleness amid the desire to have a partner, be kind to yourself and take wonderful care of yourself. Take the time to invest in an exercise program or sport you love. Try to eat good foods and not just comfort foods and sugar-filled consolation treats (I remember those late-night pints of ice cream when the phone didn't ring!). Plan a spa weekend with your best girlfriends who may also be struggling with their singleness. If you can afford it, splurge on a piece of jewelry to remind yourself you're the King's daughter and not the ugly stepsister sitting home alone after Cinderella wins the prince.

As you reflect on the current season of your life, or perhaps what it has meant for you to be single in the past, or what it means for you to wait patiently in the present, the following prayer may be helpful in conveying your heart before the Lord.

Dear Father, You know how much I want to drink of Your living water. My soul's thirst finds fulfillment only in You. Help me to remember the goodness of Your mercy, love, and graciousness to me today. But Lord, my heart longs for a companion, for a man who can hold me, comfort me, share my life and my love. Keep my heart alive to these longings without making my life conditional upon them. I ask for patience to wait on Your timing, on the right man at the right time. Thank You for this season of singleness, Lord. Give me Your confidence and security to become all that You've created me to be. Amen.

Questions and Suggestions

1. If you are presently single, where do you receive the most pressure from others about your need to find a mate—family and friends, television and movies, other singles, advertisements? How do you usually respond to this pressure?

2. If you could change one thing about yourself, what would it be? Why would you change it? How does this reflect on your present self-image? On your desire to be in a relationship?

3. Go through several women's magazines and look for articles and advertisements that tend to idealize romance and coupledom. Write in your journal about how these make you feel in comparison to your current season of life.

4. Write down the name of three people whom you trust and with whom you can share your heart. Call one of them and make an appointment for the coming week so that you can discuss areas in which you want to be held accountable. Give your friend permission to ask you the hard questions and to commit to praying for you regularly.

5. What are your areas of weakness when you're tempted to seek comfort and alleviate the pain in your life? Have you noticed any patterns in how you struggle with these temptations?

6

One Plus One:
When God Sends a Man

After I married Bishop Jakes, many single women friends began to ask me for "dating tips" and ways to attract the man of their dreams. In their minds, I had finally crossed over to the other side of life and could now speak authoritatively on how they, too, could walk down the aisle. For a couple of years, I listened to these friends and tried to suggest what I knew to be sound counsel: Be yourself, be confident in who you are, take pride in your appearance without being vain or seductive, cultivate the characteristics you want to find in your mate—honesty, humor, integrity, godliness. I'm betting you've heard these before, too. But although they're so familiar as to border on cliché, they hold true.

These were not, however, the things my girlfriends wanted to hear. They wanted to hear about a magic moment, something I said or did, something I wore or borrowed that made me irresistible. Although their heads knew better than to believe in glass slippers and diamond tiaras, their hearts were frustrated by their longing for a man and their ongoing status as single women. So, after a few years of offering the same old advice we've all heard and read about in the women's magazines, I began to speak more specifically and honestly whenever a friend asked me how to attract the man of her dreams. Most of those words I shared in the previous chapter: Look to the Lord first; don't compromise your desire for the right man; don't compromise yourself; accept your single season while keeping your heart's longings alive; be single but not satisfied. Some women told me they were downright disappointed in hearing this. They'd rather I found some trite words to provide shallow hope. But I think you know me well enough by now, dear sister, to know I couldn't play that game just to make them feel better with false hope. As much as we might long for "ten steps to finding the perfect mate," we know in our hearts that life and love don't work that way.

Love Lessons

The way love does work is often surprising and mysterious and covered in God's fingerprints. And perhaps the most mysterious aspect of it revolves around God's timing—the synchronicity of two hearts seeking Him in their lives suddenly colliding on His kingdom path. You've probably heard stories from your friends, or it may appear in your own story of coming together with your mate. But please allow me to share my own before we proceed. You may already have heard me share it before, but not quite in the way I'd like to tell it now.

In a prior chapter I spoke about what it was like to grow up in the small coalmining community where I was raised. It was a small, close-knit community, the kind where everyone knew everyone else's business. This was especially true in high school, where most of us had been together since kindergarten. As my peers and I entered the teenage years, girlhood crushes reached critical points of crisis. Would we or wouldn't we have sex with our boyfriends? As simplistic and hurtful as labeling can be, girls in my high school were on two lists: those who did and those who didn't.

Throughout high school I remained one who didn't. A shy girl who loved to read more than exercise, who wore loose dresses from the mail-order catalog, I was a "good girl." I was one of the girls whom the captain of the basketball team wanted on his arm in the daylight but not in his arms under the bleachers after dark. And, honestly, I didn't date much. Although I envied some of the beautiful, model-thin girls who went out every weekend with a different boy, I knew they were paying a hefty price by "going all the way."

When I went away to college, I discovered the world was bigger, like so many of us do when we grow into adulthood and leave our hometowns behind. On campus, with many young men and women from much larger cities and more affluent upbringings, I felt particularly self-conscious. (I tried to dress in the trendy fashions I saw other girls wearing. Thankfully, there aren't many pictures from my days in peasant blouses and bell-bottom jeans!) I began to be noticed by more young men and asked out occasionally. Soon the refrain became the same old song I'd heard before in high school: "Baby, if you love me, then don't make me wait." But although I was beginning to experiment with a few other "adult" activities, such as drinking alcohol and smoking cigarettes, I hesitated to surrender my body. I knew my body was sacred, and although my faith was fragile, I also knew God wanted me to save myself for my husband.

Eventually, though, the "if you love me" line wore down my resistance. My boyfriend said he loved me, and I was in love with the idea of someone loving me. I'll spare you the details other than to say my decision set in motion a season in my life that produced many consequences and many fears and doubts. I was learning hard lessons about love and life that only produced more questions than answers. Had I ruined the future opportunity of meeting my husband? If I did meet him now, would he still want to marry me? Could the Lord ever love me and forgive me? Could I forgive myself?

When God Sends a Man

These questions and doubts haunted me as I continued to drift along. I knew I wanted much more than just a physical connection with a man. Eventually, I found my way to a closer walk with my God and became active in a local church. A few months later, a visiting pastor spoke to our congregation and something stirred inside me like never before. This man spoke with such authority and strength; he was gifted and anointed like no one I had heard before. And he displayed gentleness and compassion. Plus—I'll say it—he was big and tall and very handsome!

In the course of his sermon, he indicated he was single.

The rest of that week, I continued to think about this man. His name was T. D. Jakes. He had grown up in a small community in West Virginia like I had, and he had lost his father at an early age, again similar to my own experience. He had a twinkle in his eye and joy in his laughter. From the modest pulpit of our church, his voice echoed like thunder one moment and soothed us like rain on a tin roof the next. He knew God's Word and had insights of wisdom far beyond his twenty-odd years.

After much prayer and deliberation, I decided to send him a secret pen-pal note. Nothing brazen or romantic, just a little note of encouragement. As I dropped it in the mail, I wondered if I'd ever hear back from him. A week later there was a reply waiting in my post office box. We began corresponding like two kids from foreign countries. The sweet spirit and boyish charm in his letters plunged my heart even deeper into the prospect of loving this man. After several exchanges, I realized I couldn't bear to continue unless he knew who I was. But that felt like such a risk. Finally, I wrote to him and revealed my secret. Would he want to meet me? Was he as attracted to my spirit as I was to his? How would he feel when he met me face-to-face?

A few days after dropping my revelation in the mail to my pen pal, I showed up for Sunday service at my church. And guess who was coming to preach revival that week? Pastor Jakes! I was thrilled and terrified at the electrifying prospect of meeting him in person. Should I go to the revival? Should I wait to see if he wrote back? Or just forget about him and move on? I decided to attend revival but then sneak out as quickly as possible afterward.

But the Lord had other plans, for as soon as the service ended that first night, my pastor's wife spotted me from across the aisle and motioned me toward her. I hesitated and measured the distance to the door. Oh, how I wished I could be invisible, dear sister! I moved forward to greet my pastor's wife, and she immediately guided me toward the front of the church. The clatter of voices simmered with after-service comments and greetings. The piano and drums lifted an upbeat hymn for us to enjoy as we lingered. Before I could believe it was true, she led me right up to our guest preacher and proceeded to introduce us.

Suddenly, I was standing before my hero. Can you imagine? Here was the opportunity, so close, and yet I was so afraid. He smiled and shook my hand as we exchanged greetings. I saw the spark of recognition as my name met his ears.

"Do you know where a bachelor can get a home-cooked meal?" he asked in earnest.

My mind raced, trying to think of how to respond. Here was a perfect opportunity—except I wasn't a very good cook! "I—I'll ask my mother," I finally stammered out. *Oh no*, I thought to myself, *I've blown it.*

But his kind eyes stayed with mine, and he nodded and began to ask me about the service, about my church, about myself. Our attraction telegraphed between us as the secret pen pals now communicated beyond words.

I was there for every night of the revival, and later in the week we shared a home-cooked meal together at my mother's. Soon the days turned into weeks, and our relationship deepened and blossomed into something alive and good. Our pen-pal correspondence turned into hours-long phone conversations. Eventually, we recognized our love for each other and discussed marriage and children, shared our thoughts on ministering together.

Now we've had over two decades together, discovering and building a deeper love for each other, raising our family, building God's kingdom, reaching out to people of all backgrounds and colors with the good news of the Father's love through the gift of His Son. And if it sounds like a fairy tale, well, it is and it isn't. There is a happily ever after quality here that I won't deny. I'm most blessed to have a man who loves God, who loves me, who is devoted to pursuing the calling our Lord has set before him. But please realize, sister, the joy borne of our relationship comes first from knowing we are in sync with God's timetable, and second from risking our hearts, including all our fears, doubts, and shame. In fact, these are the two pieces of advice I now pass on when a single friend asks about finding love. I believe these are based on more than just my own experience. I believe we can see it in one of the most romantic relationships in all of Scripture. Please allow me to explain.

Tender Hearts, Tough Times

You may recall the story of Ruth and her mother-in-law, Naomi, two women widowed and thrust together by the bonds of family and circumstance. This may not seem like the fertile ground for romance to blossom, but in God's timing you never know how He might choose to redeem our hard times. Let me remind you of their hardship before we get to the love story. After their husbands die, Naomi determined to return to her native Bethlehem and recommended that her daughters-in-law, Orpah and Ruth, remain in their native Moab. However, Ruth wouldn't hear of it. She viewed Naomi as her own family now and committed to journeying with her back to Bethlehem. Ruth said, "Entreat me not to leave you, or to turn back from following after you; for wherever you go, I will go; and wherever you lodge, I will lodge; your people shall be my people, and your God, my God" (Ruth 1:16).

I believe it worth noting even before we start that in the relationship between Ruth and Boaz we see Ruth as a compassionate woman willing to risk her heart by taking action. Now I'm not saying you should leave your job or family to follow after a man, or the hope of one, but I do believe loving someone and committing to love them has consequences. Even though Ruth sacrificed out of love for her second mother, her combined words and matching actions demonstrate her character. This is where you must begin while waiting on God's man. Then, when he arrives on the scene and you know the Lord has brought you together, you both should be willing to make sacrifices in order to continue your new journey together. I believe you will have peace about what you leave behind, even as you face the fear of an uncertain future ahead. Ruth had no guarantee, but she was willing to risk both her heart and her life circumstances.

Naomi, by contrast, struggled to risk hoping for her future. She returned to her hometown and said, "Do not call me Naomi; call me Mara, for the Almighty has dealt very bitterly with me" (Ruth 1:20). She had lost so much—she gave up her home to accompany her husband and sons to a foreign land and lost them all. Now she was returning home an old woman, with nothing to show for her life. Her bitterness had infected her ability to trust in the Lord's goodness and provision.

Ruth, however, stayed grounded in the practical concerns of finding food for the two of them. And this is where we get to the juicy part, as she encountered Boaz, a distant kinsman of her deceased husband and in-laws. Ruth discovered that it was barley harvesttime, Boaz was quite wealthy with many fields, and there was often leftover grain scattered behind the reapers. Ruth asked permission from Naomi to glean the leftover grain and to find favor with the landowner so he might provide for them. The old woman gave the younger woman her blessing and sent Ruth into the fields, where Boaz noticed her and asked after her. He must have been impressed with what he heard and saw, for he then initiated conversation with this lone, foreign woman. Let's eavesdrop on their first exchange.

> Then Boaz said to Ruth, "You will listen, my daughter, will you not? Do not go to glean in another field, nor go from here, but stay close by my young women. Let your eyes be on the field which they reap, and go after them. Have I not commanded the young men not to touch you? And when

you are thirsty, go to the vessels and drink from what the young men have drawn."

So she fell on her face, bowed down to the ground, and said to him, "Why have I found favor in your eyes, that you should take notice of me, since I am a foreigner?"

And Boaz answered and said to her, "It has been fully re-ported to me, all that you have done for your mother-in-law since the death of your husband, and how you have left your father and your mother and the land of your birth, and have come to a people whom you did not know before. The LORD repay you your work, and a full reward be given you by the LORD God of Israel, under whose wings you have come for refuge." (Ruth 2:8–12)

I find several points here worth mentioning that apply to con-temporary relationships. First, be mindful of first impressions and the reputation that precedes you. Alone in a foreign country with an old woman to care for, Ruth might justifiably have gone after a man to provide for herself and Naomi. But she didn't think this way. She didn't put her life on hold and wait for a man to find her. No, she rolled up her sleeves and struck out for the field, where she noticed unclaimed grain. Ruth was a resourceful woman, hardworking and self-sufficient without being resistant to the grace of God and others.

This reputation preceded her and was on display before the very eyes of the man who owned the fields. And he respected her hard work and willingness to take care of Naomi, something she was not beholden to do. Her kindness seems to have inspired his own. Notice how protective he was toward her, how he immedi-ately told her the "rules of the field" so she wouldn't be disre-spected or misunderstood by his young male workers. He made sure she knew where to find a cool drink and, later, where to find a midday meal.

Second, be mindful of others' kindnesses. "Why have I found favor in your eyes?" Ruth asked him. She recognized his kindness and protection. So many ladies today are often suspicious and reluctant to let a man show kindness or courtesy. I watched one young lady I know give her date a piece of her mind because he opened the door of his car for her. Now I know many feminists and strong, independent women might think I'm old-fashioned or even sexist. But I trust they will consider what I have to say with the same respect and open-minded courtesy with which I consider their viewpoints. There's nothing wrong with acknowledging, accepting, and enjoying the goodwilled kindness of a man who's both interested and interesting. I'm not talking about a man who is on a power trip and trying to make a woman feel helpless and impressed with his wealth and sophistication. Rather, we're looking for a Boaz, a kind man who takes notice of a need and offers help without any obligation or strings attached.

And what was Boaz's motive? He told Ruth she found favor because of the kindness she had shown Naomi, because of the sacrifice she made by leaving so much behind in order to care for someone in need. Whether he was attracted to her or not, he was surely impressed with her character. So impressed, in fact, he wanted to show her even more kindness.

> Now Boaz said to her at mealtime, "Come here, and eat of the bread, and dip your piece of bread in the vinegar." So she sat beside the reapers, and he passed parched grain to her; and she ate and was satisfied, and kept some back.
>
> And when she rose up to glean, Boaz commanded his young men, saying "Let her glean even among the sheaves, and do not reproach her. Also, let grain from the bundles fall purposely for her; leave it that she may glean, and do not rebuke her." (Ruth 2:14–16)

Boaz risked his generosity for this intriguing woman. He was willing to make sure she had enough to eat and enough to take home to her mother-in-law.

The Allure of Beauty

Naomi was of course impressed and delighted and explained to Ruth that Boaz was a near kinsman, one whom they could look to for family support. So Ruth continued to glean in the fields and provide for Naomi throughout the harvest season. Naomi then instructed Ruth to make the next move toward Boaz at the threshing party.

> Therefore wash yourself and anoint yourself, put on your best garment and go down to the threshing floor; but do not make yourself known to the man until he has finished eating and drinking. Then it shall be, when he lies down, that you shall notice the place where he lies; and you shall go in, uncover his feet, and lie down; and he will tell you what you should do. (Ruth 3:3–4)

Now let's pause here for a moment, girlfriend, and have a serious heart-to-heart. There are many ways to view and interpret Naomi's instruction and Ruth's obedience and consequent marriage to Boaz. Much has been made of Ruth's so-called seduction of Boaz. But I feel the word *seduction* is misused, since it's a word associated with deception and trickery, as if Ruth is casting some spell on Boaz, as if she's trying to place a Mercedes ornament on a Chevrolet hood. And that's simply not the case.

Dear reader, there's nothing wrong with wanting to look your best for your man. There's absolutely nothing to be ashamed of when you spend extra time braiding and rolling your hair in a

new style, making sure your skin is soft and smooth, and choosing a beautiful dress. My only advice here is to make it fit your
style and character. Don't try to be something you're not because
that will only confuse him. Make yourself attractive and trust the
chemistry to be there because of who you both are, not because
of extra cleavage and the color of your eye shadow.

Ruth made herself beautiful, likely with Naomi's help, and
followed through on a bold plan. She uncovered his feet and
waited there as Boaz reclined on his mat after dinner. Most
scholars agree this is a sign of physical intimacy and Ruth was
risking her reputation. But notice that Boaz was not offended
and did not misunderstand her gesture. And when she identified
herself, Boaz exclaimed, "Blessed are you of the LORD, my
daughter!" He continued by telling her not to fear, that "all the
people of my town know that you are a virtuous woman" (Ruth
3:10, 11).

There was only one thing standing in the way of Boaz's attraction to Ruth: Under Jewish law, it was customary for the near
kinsmen of a widow to have first dibs on her and on the property
of her husband. Apparently, there was a near kinsman one space
ahead of Boaz in the line for Ruth's hand. But Boaz had a plan.
He waited by the city gate, assembled a council of elders to serve
as legal witnesses, and asked the other near kinsman his intentions. The other man was not interested. So Boaz stepped in and
made his intentions clear to this other kinsman as well as the witnesses. Ruth would be his bride (see Ruth 4:1–8)!

It's striking that not only did God send a man into Ruth's life
but He sent a man of action (just as Ruth was a woman of action)
who was willing to overcome obstacles to win his woman. I wonder how Ruth felt, waiting all the while Boaz was off negotiating.
My guess is her heart was nervous but she trusted Boaz and

trusted God. Just as I imagine her heart exploded with joy when he proposed: "So Boaz took Ruth and she became his wife; and when he went in to her, the LORD gave her conception, and she bore a son" (4:13). This son was Obed, who grew up to father Jesse, the father of David. This is the lineage of God's Son, Jesus.

Through the loss and hardships Ruth endured, she worked hard and attended to the needs at hand. She sacrificed and remained kind, not bitter, expecting the Lord's goodness. She was in sync with the Lord's timing and was willing to risk her heart when God's man came along. I believe that's what He asks of each of us.

Romance and Reality

As I mentioned in introducing Ruth's story, I find it one of the most romantic in the Bible. And romance is certainly an important foundation for a relationship. However, I'm afraid some of its significance has been lost in our sex-saturated culture. So many reality shows on television play on our fascination with romance. We see bachelors and bachelorettes handing out roses to find their special someone; we see them cavorting in limousines and hot tubs and then marrying based on viewer responses. But after the season finales, after the cameras stop rolling, after the rose petals have withered and died, I wonder if any of these reality-celebrity couples have what it takes to endure.

You've likely experienced this yourself if you've been in a relationship for very long. At first it can be easy to fall in love. He calls every day, often several times a day, sends you gorgeous bouquets of flowers with sweet little notes tucked inside, buys you jewelry, and delights in taking you out and "showing you off." In return, you find yourself paying extra attention to wearing his favorite color, cooking his favorite meal for a special candlelit dinner, and slipping funny cards under his apartment door. You find yourself sneaking peeks at bridal magazines, imagining what your children might look like, and envisioning life together until old age. There's a rush, a high, that's every bit as intoxicating and addictive as the most powerful drug. Someone loves you, and you love him! And it seems as if this wonderful feeling could fuel the relationship until the end of time. You've found the man God sent your way, and this special gentleman has found you. You share the same faith, similar values, and a heartfelt desire to make a family together. All seems right with the world, no doubt.

Until reality starts creeping in and reminding you both that your relationship can't stay in this sweet, new phase for long. Talking on the phone until three in the morning is fun and utterly romantic—until you have to go in to work four hours later or get the kids off to school (not to mention fun until the phone bill arrives). It's nice to dress up and eat out in the fanciest restaurants with him—until you get a cold and want to stay at home in your sweats. Spontaneous dates add spice to your relationship—until you're gone so much there's never time for chores like dirty dishes and piles of laundry. Real life sets in and the relationship has to adapt and mature if it's going to last.

Some couples work hard to stay in this early phase of romance. Perhaps you're one of them. You continue to buy playful gifts for each other long after you've maxed out the credit cards. You use little pet names even when you're sick of them. But trying to lock the relationship into this level of relating is like trying to believe you can keep a baby from walking and growing up. Change is inevitable, and if your relationship is to survive and flourish, you must learn to change and grow with it. That's not to say you shouldn't have fun, enjoy the spontaneity of a new attraction, and revel in the joy of romance. Just don't expect it to exist at this level forever.

In fact, dear sister, I believe what we really crave is much more than just moonlight and roses. We crave the security of knowing our men will stick by us when we discover a lump in our breast, when we lose our job, or when our parents die. We want to believe they can love us without our makeup, when we burn the chicken, or when PMS makes us cranky. We long to know they will still hold us and desire us when our figures sag, when little lines sprout around our eyes, and when menopause sets in. This is when real romance kicks in! Not just the kind you see on television, but the kind that comes from a man who's willing to change a dirty diaper without being asked, capable of cooking dinner for the family when you work late, or able to surprise you with a getaway weekend he planned himself.

Now you may be saying, *But, Serita, how can I know what he'll be like in the future? How can I predict how we'll change and what his response to my needs will be?* An excellent question. My response is to consider how he treats you from the beginning. Remember that from the start, even before they married, Boaz protected Ruth and made sure she had plenty of barley.

One of the wisest proverbs I heard while growing up came from my mother: "Remember, whatever attracts you to each other in the first place will be what keeps you together in the end." At the time, I was a teenage girl unable to imagine an attraction lasting longer than that week's crush. However, as I grew older and became involved with young men, I realized that a relationship takes much more than just physical attraction and compatible personalities to survive. There's something both mysterious and comfortably mundane about those to whom we are often attracted. I find an incredible fascination in my husband that I continue to mine as we grow older together. How many facets does this man have? How does he manage to surprise me after all these years? The more I know him, the more I realize I will never exhaust this discovery process. It may sound clichéd, but it's truly like falling in love with the man all over again.

On the other hand, he seems very comfortable and even predictable sometimes. I know what meal he will enjoy when he returns home after a ministry trip. I can usually anticipate the discussion we'll have about our children. I'm familiar with the way he brushes his teeth and where he leaves his clothes lying at the end of the day. Sometimes I think I know everything about him . . . and then I'm surprised all over again and see new dimensions in him that attract me even more. This combination of solving an ongoing mystery and enjoying the familiarity of our relational home together is a powerful fuel for the longevity of our union.

Intimate History

Another quality that will help a relationship grow beyond the initial romance is the intimacy of trials suffered together, goals accomplished together, and seasons celebrated together. You've likely heard it before, dear sister, but it seems so true when considering what makes a relationship endure: The quality of time spent together makes all the difference. Certainly quantity of time affects quality, but there's no substitute for being present for one another with honesty and energy, with humor and passion. Most of us can do just fine with the romance part of the relationship. It's fun to be imaginative and receptive, to enjoy the goodies and the good times. But the follow-through after the first blush fades seems to be where many of us have trouble. It takes sacrifice. And it takes a willingness to move your expectations beyond immediate circumstances and into the long-term hope for your marriage's well-being.

Not long after my husband and I were married, he lost his job at the Union-Carbide plant. While he preached most weekends and some weeknights for revivals and other special occasions, his day job had paid our bills and helped us start our new life together. The call to ministry remained stronger than ever for him, though, and he wondered if losing his job was part of God's way of freeing him to minister full time. On the other hand, the loss hurt his pride as a husband and father who wanted to provide for his family. As our utilities were disconnected one by one, it was hard for him to feel like the man he wanted to be for us. Although it didn't occur to me at the time, I realize now that I could've complained and berated him for not bringing in more money, for not giving up his calling of ministry and finding another job, for not providing me with a nicer house and expensive clothes.

But, you see, these things were not important to me. I shared his vision for ministry and could see God's anointing on him. I knew the Lord would provide for us and see us through this tough time. I believed in him and in Him. Faith is hard to exercise when you're forced to eat at your in-laws, as we often were, and when your children think your candlelit evenings are a special occasion instead of the only light you can afford, as it was for us. But it was a small price to pay for being together as a family, for being in sync with each other and God's will, for depending on each other.

Finally, my husband received his first church. A small church in Charlottesville called him to pastor, and although it couldn't pay much and didn't have a large staff or fancy facilities, God's

Spirit was clearly in the place. After a few months, the church finally moved into a larger space, a former storefront in a rundown shopping district. We prepared for a dedication ceremony to inaugurate this new place the Lord provided for us. We wanted it to be as nice as possible, so we spent days painting and cleaning, scrubbing and sweeping, and then painting some more. My arms were terribly sore from stretching with the paint rollers. My husband seemed to be up around the clock as the special Sunday service approached. If he wasn't working to repair the light fixtures, then he was working on his sermon for the big day. I was concerned about his health, about his high blood pressure, and the toll the week's stress was taking on his body. Somehow we managed to get the place looking better than it had a right to, and on Sunday morning the place was packed as never before, folding chairs in neat rows, bodies standing in the back, and sweet music creating a wonderful mood of worship.

My husband stood at the small pulpit up front in his best and only suit and prepared to deliver his message. Only I had seen the bloody mess of his feet that morning as he tried to shove his swollen toes into his stiff dress shoes. Only I knew he had been on his feet for so long he almost couldn't stand up. Only I knew he was forced to wear his slippers as he stood up front with his feet behind the podium, smiling and welcoming the many visitors. I prayed him through that service, so afraid he would collapse from exhaustion and the toll on his body.

Several years later, as my husband walked me through the newly constructed sanctuary of The Potter's House, we marveled at what the Lord had done. We hadn't had to paint a single wall or wash down any of the molding! While we certainly contributed to its design, especially my husband with his eye for details, when he preached the first service to dedicate this new state-of-the-art ministry facility, I thanked God for the rich tapestry we had woven together in our partnership.

There is no replacement for that kind of shared history, the intimacy of such an investment. It binds us together just as your ongoing, shared history binds you and your man together. As you reflect on where you are with a particular man in your life, I encourage you to consider the following prayer.

———————————————— ᴓ ————————————————

Dear Father, thank You for all the many blessings in my life. I thank You especially right now for Your timing and for the man sent in Your season. Help me to be patient if he hasn't arrived yet. Allow me to be resourceful and confident, as Your daughter Ruth, and wait on my Boaz. When he comes, I pray that I will be willing to risk my heart and take action as necessary. And once we are together, Lord, I ask that You would give our romance a depth that would blossom into maturity for Your purposes. Allow us to support, uplift, and encourage one another just as You love us. Allow us to grow old together and develop an intimate history that withstands the storms of life. With gratitude and hope, I pray this, Father. Amen.

———————————————— ᴓ ————————————————

Questions and Suggestions

1. What kind of advice do you give to single friends? Why is it easier to seek advice about finding a mate from others than to wait patiently on the Lord's timing?

2. Recall a time or season in your life when you were afraid that you had failed in a way that would harm your future (or present) relationship with your marriage partner. How have you seen God redeem your mistake?

3. Like Ruth, in what ways have you pursued cultivating your character more than looking for a man? What trials have you endured that will make you a stronger wife, either now or someday in the future?

4. Imagine that you've been hired by your favorite women's magazine to write an article on how to find and attract your life partner. Make a list of the points you would advise your readers to consider in this pursuit. Note how many of your points reflect internal changes or responses and how many require external actions or changes.

5. What does it mean to commit to your man for the rest of your life, through good times and adversity? How can even the most difficult of circumstances—unemployment, sick children, ailing parents, overdue bills—provide you with opportunities to grow closer?

7

Love Making Love:
Sacred Sensuality

You may look at the title of this chapter and say to yourself, *Don't we hear enough about sex in our culture? What could Serita possibly have to teach me about the birds and the bees?* And you're right to question, for our media constantly saturates us with provocative images of bodies and embraces, suggestive clothing and poses. It used to focus primarily on the female form, but now, sadly enough, women have demanded their due, and there's equal exposure of the male body. And you're also right to question what I have to teach about the birds and the bees. This chapter is certainly not going to embarrass either of us by talking about techniques and Viagra.

Before I begin to address this topic directly, please allow me to share two special words. First, if you are a single lady, or currently find yourself in a season of singleness because of death or divorce, it may be very difficult to read a chapter about the wonders of lovemaking. And, certainly, my desire is not to cause you to stumble in your journey of faith. I don't want you to feel encouraged and enticed. But I don't encourage you to skip this chapter either. I believe what we're going to cover is vitally important, even if you're not ready to utilize the information at present. My special request is likely one you've heard before: Keep yourself pure and holy by abstaining from sexual relations until God sends a man to be your husband. In our present culture, I'm not sure which is more difficult: remaining a virgin or abstaining when you've known the joy of physical love before divorce or the death of your husband. In either case, I encourage you to wait patiently on the Lord and not succumb to our culture's incessant cry that in order to feel loved, attractive, or valued you must be sexually active. There is no price on your integrity, my sister.

Second, even if your physical relationship with your husband is wonderful—and if so, I applaud you—and you don't feel the need to delve into this chapter of reflection on lovemaking, I encourage you to continue reading. There is always something to be learned, even in the best of relationships. We never want to lose sight of the incredible gift of our marital intimacy or take the joy of lovemaking for granted.

Having said that, I emphasize again that I am not a therapist, counselor, or relational expert, let alone an expert on human sexuality. But in my role as wife, mother, teacher, counselor, and friend, I have seen many marriages deteriorate because the physical aspect of the relationship died long before the couple realized something was missing. The old saying about the role of sex in a marriage tends to be true: When all is well in the bedroom, sex seems to comprise only 10 percent of the relationship; when the couple aren't in the bedroom enough, sex seems to comprise 90 percent of the relationship. In other words, except for seasons of illness, childbearing, and extreme stress, a couple's sexual intimacy usually serves as a pretty good barometer of their relational health. If both partners are focused on loving and selflessly giving of themselves, both in bed and in the relationship, their partnership grows and flourishes. If both partners are focused on themselves and making sure their needs are met first, both in bed and in the relationship, the partnership will dry up and crumble.

I realize it's not usually this simple, but my observation is that most couples are probably heading in one direction or another. Or better said, the two individuals in a relationship are usually headed in one or the other direction. And when your spouse's goals and methods of attaining them, whether for sexual gratification or communication about money, differ from your own, there's going to be frustration between the sheets for you both.

Love to Love You

Depending on how long you've been married, you may feel you can skip this chapter and move right on to the next. And maybe you can. In the early stages of marriage, physical fulfillment is one of the greatest joys of being together and committed to one another. The sexual expression of love and attraction, kept inside the greenhouse of integrity and purity before the wedding, is suddenly transplanted into the rich soil of the outdoor garden of marriage and allowed to flourish. You can't wait to get home from work before your husband. You shower and change, put on some soft, easy music, and dim the lights. Your eyes meet his as soon as he walks through the door, and you want him more than anything. You're so intent on each other that you almost can't make it from the front door to the bedroom. It's easy and beautiful and effortless.

Perhaps you're reading this and remembering those times early in your relationship. And perhaps now it feels like the most difficult thing in the world to recapture. You're tired when you get home from work. He's just as tired. Kids need to be chauffeured to sports practice and then helped with homework. Dinner has to be prepared, dishes cleaned and put away. Piles of laundry await you. Bills clamor from your desk. Making love now feels like an appointment, something to check off the list so you can feel good about yourself as a wife. You've lost that lovin' feeling and don't know when it's coming back. You worry that there are plenty of other resources for him to pursue sexual gratification without you. You long for the days when it was beautiful, natural, and effortless.

Whether you're on one end of this spectrum or the other, I say that you must strive for balance on the scales of your relationship. If your love life continues to be easy, natural, and satisfying, don't overlook the other areas of growth—communication, goal setting, and spending time together with your clothes on. If, on the other hand, lovemaking has become something that requires your Daytimer and a stopwatch, then you may need to focus less on the office, the house, and the kids, and more on each other. I realize *balance* is such an elusive word. Many women hear *balance* and automatically think "perfection" or "ideal state of being." And we both know we're not going to reach that ideal state of perfection this side of heaven, dear sister.

Passionate Permission

We must live with what is realistic even as we stay focused on what matters most. Often, the first place to start is by being honest about the status of your sexual relationship. Give yourself permission to think about it, write about it in your journal, and, most important, talk about it with your husband. In fact, I would say that if I had to pick only one key to improving your lovemaking with your husband, it would be communication. Sharing your heart with him and letting him express his feelings about what you share, or don't share, in the bedroom can be one of the most beneficial conversations you'll ever have. But even before you talk to him, you will need to think through where you are in regard to this complex part of yourself and your relationship. That's why I've included this chapter—as a starting point for dealing with a crucial aspect of married life. It is not to encourage lustful temptation but to provide perspective and context to what your relationship may need, sexually speaking. Since our culture is so oversaturated with sexual images and messages, many Christian ladies run for cover to the other extreme—it's all bad, it's dirty and shameful, and it's not something to enjoy the way the world seems to revel in it.

You've heard it before, but if these feelings prevent you from facing uninhibited intimacy with your husband, you need to remember that sexuality is something from God, an incredible gift of physical pleasure, emotional connection, and psychological intimacy. It's a *good* thing! As we talked about not being satisfied with being single in an earlier chapter, I say we shouldn't be satisfied with a shameful, mediocre sex life with our spouses. Allow yourself to want more, to want the closeness and specialness of being loved by your husband in the body and personhood God created in each of you.

Part of the problem in giving ourselves permission to get honest about our sex life stems from the amount of baggage tied to sexuality. Whether single or newly married, partners for decades or married before, we all have memories and messages that make it difficult for us to view sexuality as a form of sacred sensuality. There may be abuse issues, guilt over past sexual relationships, the ongoing consequences of disease, the shadow of addictions, and painful self-consciousness over body image. It sounds simplistic, but my response is that to the extent it's possible, try to take the pressure off yourself and your spouse. Vow to begin a new season of sexual wholeness and holiness in your marriage. If that terrifies you because you've never faced the pain of your past, take just one small step and acknowledge this to your spouse. Get professional help and begin to reclaim what God intended for His children to enjoy.

Other forms of baggage may be less severe but no less problematic. We've all made mistakes, and many of them often fall in regard to our sexuality. Perhaps you feel guilty for not wanting to make love as often as he does. Maybe you haven't shared your heart with him, even though you're still offering your body. Maybe you haven't forgiven him for past grievances, which may or may not be related to the bedroom. But today is a new day, and for the sake of your marriage, as well as for each other, you must be willing to seek a new perspective on an old endeavor. A new perspective begins simply by slowing down and stepping outside the treadmill of routine activities that has trapped you. It's amazing what a long soak in a bubble bath by candlelight can do for your spirit. And then, as you relax and catch up to yourself, you can slip outside the demands of the clock and enjoy your husband's caresses. You can lose the swirling thoughts of soccer practice and overdue reports and committee meetings. You can focus not merely on the physical sensations of your sexual relationship but on the totality of your relationship, the big picture.

Two Wheels, One Direction

So much emphasis is placed on sex in our culture that it's tempting to make it the centerpiece, the hub around which the other spokes turn. But I believe it's more accurately described as the axle uniting two separate wheels into one forward-moving vehicle.

We are sexual beings, created as women and as men, undeniably. God has designed us this way. We should not try and pretend our sexuality is something disconnected from the rest of us. That's one of the main reasons our culture's obsession with sexuality is so disturbing: It objectifies and compartmentalizes one of the most personal and, as we'll explore momentarily, sacred aspects of personhood and relationship. I don't think I need to tell you that there's no switch we can flip to be suddenly in the mood, despite how badly our men sometimes wish that were true. And even though it may seem men want to have sex as if they *do* have an on/off switch, it's not the case.

Women and men are different, and that's part of what attracts us to one another. The misperception is often that men think about sex all the time and need it as they need air, food, and water. Women, on the other hand, are viewed as relational, emotional, and more interested in the attention and affirmation from their man than the act itself. Physiological differences between males and females only seem to compound the differences. As one older lady put it at a Woman to Woman marriage seminar, "Sister, my man's a microwave and I'm a slow cooker!"

I encourage you to respect the differences and make sure individual needs don't overshadow the needs of you and your partner as a couple. As my husband has observed, men feel loved when they have sex, and women feel sexy when they make love. Understand and accept that you and your partner may operate at different levels, but you share certain basic needs. These include the needs for closeness, for oneness, for true intimacy—as close as two people can be in this lifetime. Not just because your bodies are united but because hearts and spirits are in one accord as well. When this is the goal of both partners, individual needs will have no problem being met. However, if one or both of you attempt to isolate sex and focus on it for its own sake, your two wheels will get out of alignment and wobble in opposing directions. Use the differences to complement each other and meet needs only your partner can meet.

Keep the Current Flowing

How do we pursue this complementary dynamic, especially when women and men seem to have different sexual needs? As I mentioned earlier in this chapter, so much of a couple's sexuality gets tied up in knots of poor communication. It's difficult to improve, however, if you don't know your starting point and you're so inhibited by shameful baggage that you don't want to initiate the conversation. I won't pretend otherwise. But I can't stress enough that even the best marriages can benefit from a couple's sitting down and sharing their hearts about how their bodies come together in the act of lovemaking.

"But, Serita," you say, "I'd feel so embarrassed, like a schoolgirl. Or so ashamed." That may be true, but that doesn't excuse you or him from needing to talk. So many couples let their physical relationship die out because they settle for the same routine moments that were once lit by a blaze of passion and new romance. Only now the newness has worn off, and the lovemaking has become more of a chore than a privilege. If the relationship goes unchecked, and you're not willing to talk about it, don't be surprised when you are tempted by the good-looking neighbor who kindly helps you with your groceries. Don't be surprised when your husband starts working late and you suspect he's seeing someone else. Please don't get me wrong. A poor or diminished sexual relationship never justifies looking elsewhere or giving in to temptation—and I'm not saying that always happens, either. However, so much temptation could be avoided if you both were simply willing to face facts and communicate with one another regularly.

That's right—you need to talk about lovemaking with your spouse on a regular basis, not just once on your honeymoon. Your bodies change, your moods change, his seasons of life will be different from yours, events will happen that affect your sexual feelings for one another. All these items and more need to be discussed.

I recall what one older lady told a group of us at one of our Woman to WoMan conferences at The Potter's House. She shared that she felt truly blessed she and her husband had such a dynamic sexual relationship even in their golden years. When a young woman asked this sister her secret, the dear lady blushed and said that she and her husband went out to dinner once a month and had a conversation about the state of their marriage. They talked about finances, their children, their jobs, and what they needed from one another. They always concluded by talking about their bedroom.

"This kept our desire for each other fresh and pure," she said. And I'll never forget how she concluded: "If you want the water of love to stay fresh, keep the current of conversation flowing between you."

Sacred Sheets

Even when you talk openly and frequently with your partner about your sexual relationship, you still may be missing out on one of its most dynamic aspects. While you both may view the sex act as one of deep intimacy and closeness, you may not realize it also has great capacity to draw us closer to the Lover of our souls, our Father God. As we join our bodies with one another, we are moving outside our aloneness and uniting with our lover, our partner, our soul mate—and experiencing an acceptance that reflects God's unconditional love and grace. You see, what happens between the sheets is sacred. Our Creator made us this way and intended the act to be holy and honoring of Him. I believe this is why He compares the relationship between a man and wife to Christ's relationship to the church, His bride. This is why we are instructed to regard our bodies as temples of the Holy Spirit and to be careful how we use them. Let's consider this instruction together in order to appreciate the sacred quality of our sexuality.

> Now the body is not for sexual immorality but for the Lord, and the Lord for the body . . .
>
> Do you not know that your bodies are members of Christ? Shall I then take the members of Christ and make them members of a harlot? Certainly not!
>
> Or do you not know that he who is joined to a harlot is one body with her? For "the two," He says, "shall become one flesh."
>
> But he who is joined to the Lord is one spirit with Him.
>
> Flee sexual immorality. Every sin that a man does is outside the body, but he who commits sexual immorality sins against his own body.
>
> Or do you not know that your body is the temple of the Holy Spirit who is in you, whom you have from God, and you are not your own?
>
> For you were bought at a price; therefore glorify God in your body and in your spirit, which are God's. (1 Corinthians 6:13, 15–20)

This passage may seem to condemn sexuality, but that's not the case at all. In fact, it's condemning immorality—misusing sexuality by joining oneself to a prostitute. By comparison to what is acceptable and good in the Lord's sight, Paul cites the passage from Genesis 2:24 in which the Creator blesses His creation, Adam and Eve. God Himself chose to make Eve from the flesh and bone of Adam so when they made love it would be like a part of each other finding itself in its mate. The human body is holy by virtue of its creation in the image of God. When we are believers, we are indwelt with the living power of God's Holy Spirit. If we cheapen our sexuality by overlooking its spiritual dimension, or by violating it by hooking up with an old boyfriend or a good-looking coworker, then we are sinning against God as well as our spouse. When God gifts us with a partner, He wants us to delight in each other, to share in the sensual wonders of His creation.

Better than Wine

As we've just discussed, sexual oneness reflects spiritual oneness, and if you focus only on having a better sex life through new positions you read about in a magazine at the salon, or on wearing a new brand of lingerie, you may not be addressing the real problem. On the other hand, if you feel that you and your husband are one in the spirit but struggle to keep the sparks alive in your physical relationship, time alone with the atmosphere of candles and music may be in order. For some couples, especially those strong in the faith, it can be a challenge to let their hair down and thoroughly enjoy the physical pleasures of lovemaking. But we are called to love making love, not to dread it or feel ashamed of it. As Paul wrote in another letter to one of the early churches, "Let the husband render to his wife the affection due her, and likewise also the wife to her husband. The wife does not have authority over her own body, but the husband does. And likewise the husband does not have authority over his own body, but the wife does" (1 Corinthians 7:3-4).

Many ladies I talk to tell me they have so much baggage related to their bodies and sexuality, they feel guilty, dirty, and ashamed to acknowledge God's presence in lovemaking. Aware of past encounters or abuse, or afraid of their own inadequacies, they're afraid to risk their hearts with their bodies before their lover. If you have felt this way, it may be helpful to discuss these issues with your mate at a time when you're not in bed attempting to be intimate. You must realize, too, the enemy will resort to any means to undermine your marriage, and shame is often one of his favorite weapons.

I believe the best way to overcome such shame is to remind yourself of two things. First, as we've seen, remember that lovemaking in marriage is holy, created and ordained by God as His gift, and honors Him. It's not just procreative to make children, or recreative to feel good together, it's be-creative, a sacred and mysterious part of being whom God made you to be. Second, practice accepting your mate as you want to be accepted in the total context of your relationship, not just as some body you're going to lie down beside. This is where our culture places another barrier to the ongoing sexual health of a married couple. As we've mentioned several times, the emphasis on television and in the movies, in advertisements and magazines, is on youthful perfection. Don't get hung up on looking perfect or expecting him to look like Denzel Washington or Brad Pitt. Instead, focus on the special qualities that are uniquely his. Accept him as you want to be accepted, loved because of who you are and not just what you look like.

Allow yourself to revel in the feel of his hands on your shoulders. Taste the sweetness of his kiss. These are not lines from some romance novel. These are from God's Word. In Song of Solomon, we see an extraordinary description from the Shulamite woman and her Beloved. She says, "Let him kiss me with the kisses of his mouth—for your love is better than wine" (1:2). To which he replies, "Behold, you are fair, my love! Behold, you are fair! You have dove's eyes . . . Like a lily among thorns, so is my love among the daughters" (1:15; 2:2). The lovely, dark-skinned Shulamite then states, "Like an apple tree among the trees of the woods, so is my beloved among the sons. I sat down in his shade with great delight, and his fruit was sweet to my taste" (2:3). Can't you feel the sensuality of these words as they roll off the tongues? Love is better than wine, indeed!

Secrets of Sensuality

Lovers are called to cherish their beloved in special ways and special places. If it's been a long time since the two of you were alone together, find a way to make time together a priority. Prepare yourself for a new season of joy as you delight in sensual closeness to your man. The Shulamite woman was called by her beloved to a season of new birth, new beauty, and sweet intimacy.

> Rise up, my love, my fair one,
> And come away.
> For lo, the winter is past,
> The rain is over and gone.
> The flowers appear on the earth;
> The time of singing has come,
> And the voice of the turtledove
> Is heard in our land.
> The fig tree puts forth her green figs,
> And the vines with the tender grapes

Give a good smell.
Rise up, my love, my fair one,
And come away!
O my dove, in the clefts of the rock,
In the secret places of the cliff,
Let me see your face,
Let me hear your voice;
For your voice is sweet,
And your face is lovely. (2:10–14)

Notice the unashamed appeal to the senses in this beautiful poem. Yes, even the form in which it's written is one reserved for special, often love-inspired, communication. The language is beautiful and the images fresh and lovely. Can you hear the singing and the cooing of the turtledoves? Can you smell the fresh blossoms of springtime? Can you grasp the rough facets of rock within the secret fortress of your relationship?

I encourage you to realize that the winter of individual loneliness has ended, and the spring of joyful togetherness has begun. This realization is often difficult to maintain in our hectic, hurry-up world. We struggle to focus on the present moment, on the beauty of our Lord's creation in the world around us, and most of all on each other. Dear lady, stop for a moment and think about the last time your mind was free and your senses fully engaged.

If you and your mate lack that extra spark, or even if things are going well and you simply want to maintain the blaze of passion, I encourage you to set aside some alone time, drop the kids off with Grandma or with friends, and then prepare to read Solomon's Song to one another. Unplug the phone, turn off the cell phone, lock the PDA away. Put on some favorite music, draw a bath, and light some candles. Wear his favorite perfume or a new fragrance that will soon become memorable. Rediscover what it was that attracted you to him in the first place. Allow yourself to melt in his arms as you did on your honeymoon. You might be surprised at the freedom you experience when you allow yourself permission to enjoy the pleasure God intended. If you love to make love, then your marriage relationship will be like a garden. If the ground is tilled and the seeds planted, watered, and blessed with sun, the fruit produced will be beautiful, sensual, delicious, and nourishing.

Perhaps this chapter has been difficult for you. As we've seen, we can't disconnect the sexual aspect of your relationship from the rest of its components. We must not lose sight of its sacred and holy dimensions, nor should we diminish God's intentions by minimizing its incredible beauty and sensuality. Every relationship goes through seasons, and perhaps it would be helpful to talk with your mate and identify where you've been with regard to your love life. You might consider using the following prayer as a way of rekindling the passion in this area of your life.

Dear Creator of all that is lovely and beautiful, I thank You for the gift of my body and for the incredible gift of my husband. We desire to honor You in our relationship and to enjoy the goodness You have presented to us in each other. I pray that we may always remember the holiness of our lovemaking, the sacred way it represents Your beloved Son, and us His church. May we also not be ashamed to reclaim some of the joy You bestowed on Adam and Eve as they enjoyed oneness in Your Garden. Allow us to embrace the sensual fruits reserved for Your children in the marriage bed. Give us patience and acceptance for one another. Allow us to love one another as You love us. Amen.

Questions and Suggestions

1. How would you describe your attitude as you started this chapter? How important do you believe lovemaking is to the life and health of a marriage? Why?

2. What are the barriers you face when you consider addressing your sexual relationship with your husband? Busyness? Exhaustion? Fear? Lack of communication? Past baggage? All of the above? Others?

3. Read this chapter together with your husband. Discuss the way you each feel after each section and which points most accurately describe your present relationship. Ask each other what you'd like to see change in the bedroom and then make a plan about how to change it. Spend some time together praying for all dimensions of your relationship, including the sexual one.

4. Why do you suppose God designed us to be sexual beings? How does lovemaking reveal aspects of His character? What are those specific aspects that are revealed?

5. Make a list of things you can do for your husband to make him feel loved and cherished outside of the bedroom. Choose one of these items to do for him without letting him know beforehand.

❧ 8 ❧

Seasons of His Life:
Growing Closer Through Life Changes

The church sanctuary looked like a greenhouse, bedecked with bouquets of beautiful roses, lilies, and orchids. We guests packed the pews in our best summer dresses and suits, contentedly listening to the beautiful music from the string ensemble until the magic moment arrived. Then the familiar strains of the wedding march began, and we all rose and turned to watch the gorgeous bride take her traditional walk down the aisle. Her attendants were already assembled before her down at the altar and now her groom emerged to take her hand from her father.

As I was privileged to share in this wonderful ceremony recently, and to hear my husband officiate, I was struck by the truth and power contained in the traditional wedding vows. "For richer or poorer, in sickness and in health, till death do us part." My thoughts were twofold that day as I watched these two beautiful young people begin their married life together. First, most of us have no idea what those vows will look like as they're refined through the fire of daily trials and life circumstances. Second, from the depths of living out these vows will come a woman's greatest opportunities to support and stand beside her man. Certainly our lives change—and we'll address some of the specific life stages and transitions that we experience as women later in the book. However, knowing what to expect as we watch our men go through transitions, and the unique ways in which we can support them, can make a world of difference in the quality of our male relationships. Let's explore some of the various ways we can live out our vows with our husbands as well as offering support and encouragement to the other key men in our lives during seasons of change.

Impossible Dreams

One of the simplest and most primary ways we support our men throughout our lives together emerges in how we nurture his dreams. Can you think back to some of those late-night conversations the two of you used to have when you were dating or newly married? You planned out your entire life together as you sat out under the stars or in the all-night coffee shop. You imagined how many children you wanted to have and what their names would be. You envisioned the kind of house you wanted to share together and how to make it your home. And somewhere in these discussions, you began to see a part of him you'd never seen before. His heart lowered its defenses, and suddenly he began pouring out his dream for fulfilling his calling and the lifestyle he wanted to attain through his success. Whether he dreamed of pastoring his own church, like my husband, or wanted to start his own business, pursue his talent as a singer, or start a farm raising apples in the Midwest, you noticed the gleam in his eye and the rush in his voice.

Truth be told, you may have thought it was the craziest, most surprising thing he could have come up with. *A professional baseball player?* you perhaps thought to yourself. *A chain of your own restaurants?* You may have had serious doubts about the feasibility of such high hopes as he revealed them to you. And you may still harbor doubts about the realistic part of what he wants to attain. However, your response is not about what circumstances have to happen in order for his dream to fall into place. Save those conversations for the bankers, investors, collaborators, and mentors in his life. No, your response is all about your belief in *him*. No matter how far-fetched, how crazy, how out-of-this-world his dream may sound, what he's really asking you is this: Will you labor beside me as I risk pursuing something in which I might fail? Will you still love me whether I force us into bankruptcy chasing this dream or whether I make us richer than kings if it succeeds? Will you truly love me through the ups and downs of this crazy roller-coaster ride we just started together?

Certainly I knew my husband was called to the ministry when I married him. He shared his conviction of God's calling with me, and evidence of his anointing was more than clear for me to see as I sat in the congregation and listened to him preach. However, his vision of where God was calling him next has not always been so easy for me to see. Not long after we were married, my trust in him was put to the test. In addition to his duties as pastor, my husband was also working a day job to pay the bills. At the same time, the church he was pastoring continued to grow; we clearly needed a new facility. In the midst of searching for new properties for our church, my husband lost his other job. After much prayer and many late-night conversations, he felt the Lord was providing this season to free him for full-time ministry. Despite the uncertainty with our finances, I agreed and felt perfect peace about where the Lord was calling us.

The reality of full-time pastoring soon set in. Long hours and uncertain pay, along with the growing church's need for a new site, made for a stressful transition. Nonetheless, my husband held to his vision and continued searching tirelessly for just the right spot. I'll never forget when he came home one evening and said, "I found it! Come on, I'll take you there."

When we first visited a vacant, run-down movie theater on the outskirts of town, where he envisioned a growing, thriving church, I couldn't see it the way he could. My vision was a bit limited by the gaping holes in the floor and ceiling, by the years of decay and dirt encasing the rotted seat cushions, by the remains of sticky sweets and the litter of old popcorn bags. But my husband led me by the hand and pulled me from corner to corner of that run-down property, declaring, "And we can put the choir up here, and the pulpit right here. Maybe we'll set up the piano right over there. And we can have the kids' classes right back over there," and on and on, as excited as an architect designing a grand sanctuary on the choicest site. I trusted his vision because I love him and believe in him. I participated in fulfilling his vision because I trust in God's ability to bring impossible dreams to life.

Knowing how to respond to our men's dreams is a tricky thing, dear lady. Certainly, there are times when we must be the voice of reason, the voice of balance and practicality. That's what my mind wanted as I wondered how in the world the run-down theater could ever be cleaned up and turned into a respectable meeting place for a growing church. But my heart knew my good man's vision was unstoppable. He had a calling from God and a strong vision for God's work housed in this abandoned place. As I moved from the land of logical responses into the territory of my own heart, it didn't really matter whether or not we succeeded or failed. As long as I was with him and we were united as a team, as long as I was as convinced as he was we were pursuing God's dream and not just our own flights of fancy, I was at peace. Because I believed in him, and because I trusted God, I could risk failing and let go of whatever fears and uncertainties I faced. No, it's not easy, but living a life of faith in relationships with other people will never be easy.

One great resource from which I continue to draw strength when it feels frightening to support my husband's dreams is God's Word. Consider some of the impossible dreams God fulfilled in Scripture. He makes it clear that He enjoys displaying His glory by making the things that are impossible with men possible through His power. The story of Noah comes to mind as one of these instances. Let's explore the impossible dream he was charged with bringing to life:

> So the LORD said, "I will destroy man whom I have created from the face of the earth, both man and beast, creeping thing and birds of the air, for I am sorry that I have made them."
> But Noah found grace in the eyes of the LORD . . .
> And God said to Noah, "The end of all flesh has come before Me, for the earth is filled with violence through them; and behold, I will destroy them with the earth. Make yourself an ark of gopherwood; make rooms in the ark, and cover it inside and outside with pitch . . . And behold, I Myself am bringing floodwaters on the earth, to destroy from under heaven all flesh in which is the breath of life; everything that is on the earth shall die. But I will establish

My covenant with you; and you shall go into the ark—you, your sons, your wife, and your sons' wives with you. And of every living thing of all flesh you shall bring two of every sort into the ark, to keep them alive with you; they shall be male and female." (Genesis 6:8, 13–14, 17–19)

Can you imagine the conversation Noah must have had with his wife after he finished talking to God? "Honey, pack your things, 'cause we're going on a cruise!" No, I don't imagine that's quite the approach he took. He had to explain to his wife that God had spoken to him and shared the impending destruction of the entire world. Then he had to convince her that his part in all this was to build an ark so they could survive with their children and their children's spouses. And on top of that, they also had to become temporary zookeepers by including a pair of every living creature on the earth in their new floating home!

Now certainly Noah's wife must have been a woman of faith and must have supported her husband in his calling, but I think I would have had second thoughts myself.

We don't know for sure, but Noah's vision likely went against the circumstantial evidence of the time, with the exception of the corrupt evil surrounding them. But it seems likely that it wasn't raining or flooding when he began building the ark. He likely endured some measure of ridicule from the wicked people on whom God had given up. It was an extraordinary measure of faith for this man to build a huge boat and prepare for a flood that hadn't even started. We aren't told how Noah's wife responded, but she was clearly on board the ark when the time came: "So Noah, with his sons, his wife, and his sons' wives, went into the ark because of the waters of the flood" (Genesis 7:7). Perhaps she had her doubts, just as I had mine about renovating the old theater into our church building. But it seems evident she was compelled to trust her husband's dream and his calling because she believed in him and she trusted God.

As I've continued to support my husband's life calling and as I've talked with other women, I've realized God rarely gives one partner a vision and calling without sharing it with the other partner. We may not like it, we may not understand it, but it's usually undeniable. When we sense His presence in the midst of those seasons of pursuing dreams, we can face down our fears and join in the excitement of watching the impossible birthed into being. Even when the venture fails or does not go as planned, we must keep our faith in our husbands alive. This is where our trust in God eclipses the circumstances that make our man's dream appear to have died. This is where we demonstrate our unconditional love and support for him, regardless of the outcome. We trust that God had a purpose in leading him down this road, even if it appears to be a blind alley right now. Overall, as long as we convey our belief in him, we will grow together through the pursuit of his dreams, and not apart.

Lost Causes

Some of the hardest times in any relationship will occur when you share seasons of loss together. Whether it is the death of a dream when your business fails, your home going up in smoke, the loss of a child to illness or gangs, or the passing of a beloved parent, these massive blows will reconfigure your entire world. It's as if the jigsaw-puzzle picture that was just coming into clear focus has been blown apart and forced into a new and confusing form. Individuals, even while sharing the same loss, may deal with their grief in different ways. Stereotypically, men have more trouble expressing their emotions of loss and pain when faced with such calamity. Women, on the other hand, supposedly are freer with their emotions and more willing to convey their heartache.

This may or may not be the case with you and your mate. You may struggle to express your difficult emotions more than he does. Regardless of your individual modes of expressing sadness, when you share a mutual loss of this magnitude, the key is not to allow grief to separate and isolate you. This is when you must speak your heart to one another, cry together, scream together, and pray together for the strength to persevere. Even if the two of you consider yourselves very private people, you must still realize that the loss belongs to both of you. You must also be careful not to blame one another. Chances are that both of you feel some degree of guilt over the loss, as if you could have prevented it if you had chosen differently or acted sooner. These are normal, very human responses, but you must not allow them to drive a wedge between the two of you. When there's silence and unexpressed emotions between you, it's like static buildup—the longer you wait, the greater the charge when you finally attempt to connect. If you wait too long, the electric shock may be too much to keep your relationship alive.

In other seasons of life, you will watch your husband endure losses that are more uniquely his own. You will certainly have a stake in them, of course, for whatever he loses, you lose as well. However, when the loss affects him more personally or directly, you will be forced to offer him support and comfort only you can provide. This will certainly vary from couple to couple and from one loss to another. But there are some ways you can help him move through these dark periods of his life. These may seem obvious or difficult to pin down into a how-to formula, but they're gifts we must be aware of our husband needing from us. Let's examine a few of these unique ways a woman can support and comfort the men in her life. While I'm thinking primarily of ways a wife can give to her husband, most of the strategies can be applied to helping your father, brothers, sons, and male friends deal with their grief as well.

Give him ownership. Perhaps the place to begin is simply to acknowledge that his loss is uniquely his. Despite how it may affect you, how well you relate to it from your personal losses, or what you may have lost as well, you need to respect his very personal stake in the person, dream, or opportunity that has now passed him by. As I watched my husband go through the tremendous loss of his mother, I was struck by how acutely aware he was of his own pain. While I shared much of his grief over losing this beloved woman, I knew that I couldn't share in his loss in exactly the same way. She was his dear friend and greatest supporter, the woman who had birthed him and believed in his giftedness long before I came onto the scene. Even though I had lost a parent before, no one's experience is identical to anyone else's. So despite my best attempts to grieve with him, I sensed how terribly alone and sad he felt. While comforting him, I allowed him to own it as uniquely and personally his.

Give him a place to grieve. The next gift we can offer is a safe place in which he can express all that he feels, no matter how crazy, how raw, how out of character it may seem for him to express his heart. This may involve time alone for the two of you to talk, to get away, or to sit in silence together. While my husband certainly did not need my permission to express his feelings, what I found was that he often felt more at ease in doing so when I encouraged him to let loose and pour out the bitter acid of loss from his heart. As I've talked with other ladies, I've found this is often something we can do for our men when they face a season of loss. If we help them make a space in their life for this pain, they often are more willing to share it with us, to speak it and move through it. Otherwise, the tendency is for them to bottle it up inside and wait for it to explode in other arenas of their life. Indeed, I believe this is one of the leading causes of men's midlife crises. They have so much unexpressed grief, anger, and sorrow over their life's losses and nowhere and no one to give them room to express it.

Comfort him in the little things. Another way to support your man through a painful season is by pampering him. Certainly we try to show attention and spoil him in loving ways day in and day out, but during the stress and ache of a grieving period, it helps if you can give him extra attention and provide more comfort. Whether it's removing other stressors from his life—the bills, the children, the chores—or whether it's providing more comfort—his favorite foods, hobbies, or lovemaking—I encourage you to be sensitive to his needs. I caution you as well not to overlook your own needs during these seasons. Make sure you're not comforting him to the devastation of your own soul's needs.

Give him a room of his own. Another suggestion is to be sensitive to his moods and know when to give him his own space.

There will be times when he wants to pour out his heart and talk for hours, and other times when he may simply want you to hold him and not let go. Then there will be times when he's indifferent, aloof, and downright hostile to you and your attempts at comfort. He may feel embarrassed by his own intense emotions, or about having shared them with you. In light of his present loss, he may be so afraid of losing you someday that he resents growing closer as you comfort and soothe him. Or he may simply need some time away, alone or with other men. Don't take it personally. Simply remember that this season will pass and he will again crave your companionship.

Give him a Boys' Night Out. Finally, allow him to share his experience of grief with other men in his life. After my dear mother-in-law passed away, I realized my husband often felt that he was being weak if he continued to display his emotions to me. He clearly wanted to connect with other men who had experienced the loss of their mothers and had felt some of the things he was now feeling. As the initial waves of shock and grief subsided a bit, I realized how much he was in the process of totally re-seeing himself and his world. He often wanted and needed my comfort and point of view. But he also needed and wanted the support of Christian brothers and faithful friends who could offer a different kind of comfort and support. So I encouraged him to have a boys' night out—to go see an action/adventure movie or comedy, go bowling, take in a ball game, or go joyriding in a rented convertible. Feeling more maternal than I cared to, I asked him to promise me he'd be careful and to let me know when to expect him back. Otherwise, I told him to have a good time and enjoy being off duty. As long as you're communicating together and he's sharing something of his heart and needs, and not using his male friends to shut you out, I believe his time with them can be invaluable.

Growing Pains

While the losses and hardships of life are obvious seasons when we can support our spouse, there are other seasons when wonderful things happen that nonetheless throw him for a loop. A hard-earned promotion, an inheritance, an upturn in his business, the completion of a college degree, a move to another city are all worth celebrating even as they bring changes and seasons of new responsibilities and expectations. Depending on his personality and temperament, it may be hard for him to enjoy this new success. He may be so driven that he's constantly on to the next challenge, the next deadline, the next goal to be met. Often the best way for you to support him through this season is to slow him down and help him realize what an amazing accomplishment he's privileged to enjoy. Whether it's throwing a congratulatory party, helping him choose a reward for his hard work, taking him out for a special dinner, or giving him a special gift appropriate to his new season, you can allow him to have perspective and appreciate the milestone he's reached.

You may need to give him room to grow into his new position. Continue to encourage him and boost his confidence regarding his accomplishment, even as you share in helping him set future goals. I've often observed that many wives are so intimidated by their husband's success or newfound wealth that they no longer feel needed. Trust me, no matter how much he succeeds or how much money he makes, he still needs you and values what you think of him.

As he changes and grows in new directions, don't be afraid to grow and change yourself. He's often been working hard so he can provide for you and allow you to experience new opportunities. Remind him that he needs to enjoy the perks of his accomplishment as much as you do. So if he wants you to splurge on a vacation or on help around the house, and you can afford it, then do so. Use the extra time to take care of yourself and to plan ways you can enjoy time with him.

Rhythms of Life

Perhaps the most challenging transitions are the ones inherently natural to the course of your relationship: adjusting to married life, having children, finding the right career niche, raising your children, reaching midlife, becoming empty nesters, enjoying your retirement and the golden years. These are changes that you will undergo together, yet his experience of them might be very different from your own. As we've mentioned before, you may need to adjust to new ways of relating as the seasons of your life change.

In the early months of newly married life, you may both have a lot to learn. Perhaps you need to work on communication skills and conflict resolution. It takes some getting used to one another and learning each other's little habits and quirks. He may have issues with past relationships or a divorce he's still working through. Perhaps the best way to encourage him to process these issues is through talking to you and to his male friends. Premarital counseling can certainly head off many of these problems, but it may need to be continued after the honeymoon as you adjust to one another.

As you pursue starting a family, you must realize that while your body has nine months to prepare you for the arrival of your new edition, he may not be quite as prepared. He may worry that he will lose you—your time, your attention, even your body—to this new little stranger. He may also be worrying about the kind of father he will be because of past issues with his own father. You may need to reassure him that as long as he loves this baby, most of fathering will fall into place.

Later, after the baby has arrived, you will both be adjusting to a new season of late nights and early mornings, of diaper changes and frequent feedings. Don't lose sight of each other in the midst of this exhilarating and exhausting time. Allow him to learn as much as possible about how to care for the baby—to feed, change, and bathe her. Once the child is old enough to be left with a grandparent or close friend, surprise him with a romantic date night, something special for the both of you.

As the children grow, and as his or both of your careers take off, you may need to help remind him about how much his presence is needed in the children's lives. Don't nag, but do encourage him to volunteer at their school, drive the car pool occasionally, and attend their games and concerts. Don't set him up to be just the phantom provider who never participates but is always quick with provision.

I recall one dear couple whom my husband and I counseled together during a rocky part of their marriage. At one point, as we discussed the division of roles between them, the husband concluded, "I'm just the cash cow!" To which his wife added, "Well, then, I'm the pack mule!" Both of them felt they had been reduced to either providing or homemaking. They had lost their sense of what it meant to raise a family together and how to keep their relationship intact.

Much is made of the so-called male midlife crisis (we'll talk later about our own such phase). As I've mentioned, I believe much of the reason men suddenly seem to wake up one morning and want a drastic change in their lives stems from their unwillingness to deal with their life losses and disappointments. The other major contributor, of course, is a keen awareness of their body's decline and their impending mortality. The psalmist wrote, "My life fades like a shadow at the end of day and withers like grass" (102:11 CEV). As he begins to lose people he loves—his parents, friends, business partners—this truth sinks into his bones, and suddenly he realizes he is on the front lines. His parents can no longer protect him. His body is no longer invulnerable. He can't throw the ball as far, run as fast, or recover as quickly as he once did. This can be a rude awakening to many gentlemen, and they often attempt to combat it through denial, association with youth, or, in the best situation, by embracing more of their faith and God's calling to authenticity.

Denial is perhaps the hardest to deal with from a wife's point of view. He tries to pretend he's young again—in the way he dresses or cuts his hair or the car he drives. He may pay more attention to younger women and seem more preoccupied with sex. It's almost as if he believes he can rejuvenate himself if he associates with younger people and their status symbols and toys. This can be very difficult for you, as someone who loves him, to weather. If you're not willing to play your part and fuel his fantasy, there will be conflict.

My best advice here is to remain true to yourself and

gently remind him of who he is. This doesn't mean he can't change or have a makeover or new car. It simply means he shouldn't try to find his worth in things or make them more important than what's going on inside him. If you can remind him of his core passions and beliefs and then find ways to get him plugged back into them, often a midlife crisis can be a beautiful beginning to a new, more authentic season of your marriage. No more pretense or games. No more trying to keep up with others or worrying about what they think. Instead, you'll find he's more real with you than ever before, more open with his emotions, and more self-confident in his preferences and decisions.

Finally, as your children grow into young adults and leave your home, you will be faced with seeing him again as if for the first time. Suddenly your roles as Mommy and Daddy are pulled out from under you, and you're forced to get reacquainted with one another. This can be one of the greatest, most challenging turning points in a marriage. It's certainly shocking when we see couples who have been together for twenty, twenty-five, thirty years or longer suddenly divorce, but often they did not allow themselves to change once they were alone and faced with their spouse again. While he may be the same man you married those many years ago, he has changed, and so have you. Dear sister, don't try to force him to be someone he was decades ago! Allow yourself to get familiar all over again. He has new preferences, new ideas, and new feelings you never discovered while the kids were growing up. Invite him to share himself with you as if you're just meeting for the first time. Look for those elements that first attracted you to him and see how they've evolved. Allow him to get to see how you've changed as well. Face the fear of not knowing each other and start introducing yourselves.

No matter what stage of life you find yourself in at present, you are uniquely qualified to support and encourage the men in your life. Whether you're newly married or celebrating your golden anniversary or somewhere in between, I encourage you to give thanks for all the men in your life, especially if there's one the Lord has chosen as your husband. I would be remiss if I didn't close this chapter by emphasizing the most important gift you can give the men in your life: prayer. Offering up daily prayers for the men in your life and their needs is one of the strongest, most effective strategies for loving and supporting them. Perhaps the following prayer can help you convey your hopes and desires for your current relationships with men, or you may want to direct it specifically around your husband.

Dear God, I am most grateful for all the special men You have placed in my life right now. I give You thanks for each one of them and ask Your special blessing on their hopes and dreams. Please allow me to be an encourager, a supporter, someone who believes in them and labors alongside them in the pursuits to which You have called us. As they endure various changes and transitions in their lives, please allow me to grow with them and know how to love and support them. Give me wisdom and discernment so I can nurture their dreams, soothe their hurts, comfort their hearts, and meet their needs according to Your purposes. Keep us strong, and help us always to seek You first as we persevere in the faith. Amen.

Questions and Suggestions

1. Why is it significant that wedding vows usually include the extremes of life—wealth and poverty, sickness and health—in the commitment they express? How do these extremes help prepare a couple for their life together?

2. How would you describe the changes you and your husband have shared together? How did these transitions affect your relationship?

3. If you're married, look over your wedding photos and recall the wonderful memories of that special day. If you have a copy of your wedding vows (or can transcribe them form the video or from memory), read through them and reflect on the extremes you've endured so far. Share your thoughts with your husband when you get the next opportunity.

4. How have the men in your life responded to the big losses they've suffered? How have they allowed you to share their grief and comfort them? What do you wish you could do differently for them than you've done so far?

5. In which "rhythm of life" season do you find yourself in presently? What are the unique challenges in your relationship during this present season? How could you use these to draw closer to your husband?

$\mathscr{P}$ART 3

I Stand Beside Him:
Seeing Yourself
in the Spotlight

9

Equal Billing:
Two Leads in One Show

The auditorium is filled to capacity with shimmering dresses, ebony tuxedos, and glittering jewels. Elegant women with beautifully coiffed hair sit next to strong, handsome men, each holding their breath to see who will win the night's golden prize. It's difficult to discern who is the star and who is the behind-the-scenes supporting spouse—some couples shine equally bright, with both husband and wife individual stars in their own right, uniting to form a Hollywood dream combination.

We see these couples each year at events such as the Academy Awards, where accomplishments are recognized in a number of categories reflecting excellence in the motion picture industry. The two most important are offered in two categories for both men and women: Best Supporting Actor and Best Actor in a Leading Role. Often these distinctions seem interchangeable. An actress may be nominated as a supporting player for a film in which she has more lines than someone else's role nominated as a leading role. This makes me wonder. Is supporting determined only by how much on-screen, out-front time a player has? Is a leading role shaped only by those who demand the spotlight? And better yet, what happens when you have two Oscar-winning performances from both the male and female lead? Who gets top billing?

As I've watched these award shows, I've often imagined the response if some normal women from everyday life were given the applause, the recognition, and the award statuette for Best Wife in a Supporting Role or Best Leading Lady in the role of wife and mother. Wouldn't that be enjoyable? Perhaps it might make amends for the many women who have been, and some who still are, overlooked for their contributions. In the "good old days" of our mothers and grandmothers, men were usually the ones out front on life's stage receiving prizes, while the women stayed behind the curtain supporting and nurturing, caring for the home and the children, and working for their family. Often the women worked harder than the men to keep the bills paid and the family together. However, no matter how much they contributed, they were always viewed as supporting players, not the leads.

Times have changed, thankfully. Women and men can now respect and support each other in their shared mutual goals of making a home together and providing for their family. Women are often in the spotlight alongside their men; some may even have a more public starring role than their husbands who support them from backstage. Indeed, as I mentioned at the beginning of this book, the old adage observing that "Behind every good man stands a good woman" has become "*Beside* every good man stands a good woman."

However, it's often hard to dance standing side by side. As a relationship progresses, the line between supporting and leading roles is one that you and your husband must learn to negotiate together. You both will have to learn how to keep your love alive as the romance matures over time within the circumstances of everyday life. Some seasons will see you feeling like the supporting partner, encouraging, nourishing, and reinforcing his dreams and desires. He may go out into the bright lights of the world each morning leaving you home in the shadows of childcare and housekeeping. Other times will find you in life's spotlight, excelling and achieving, while he offers you the confidence and support you need. You'll be dazzling the public eye with your talents, style, and abilities, while he keeps the home fires burning. Some of you will experience parallel paths with your spouse as your meteoric success streaks alongside his stellar accomplishments.

While each partnership will require different dance steps, some responses to life's music remain basically the same. If you're to maintain the loving commitment to the health of your marriage and know how to stand alongside your man, you must focus on the priorities of a balanced marquee. From my own experience, I want to focus on the three vibrant areas of your relationship most prone to causing conflict and imbalance in your marriage: accepting your husband's covering, avoiding competition, and advancing communication. The first area refers to respecting the basic differences between men and women as God created us and exploring the complementary contributions both husbands and wives are called to invest in a well-balanced partnership. The second area examines what it means for us to stay united in common goals rather than be divided by individual agendas. This third area may seem obvious, but is an essential lifeline to the other areas and to the overall well-being of your marriage. Let's begin by considering some foundational aspects of what it means to share the billing as wife and husband.

Suffocation or Security

Even though I am a bit old-fashioned about what it means to be a woman, and the way a wife contributes as a keeper of the home and mother of children, I'm progressive enough to know that it takes equality in the relationship for the marriage to adapt to life's roller-coaster circumstances. No matter how much a lady stays out of the public eye, her partner and family know the leading role she plays and honor her accordingly. The kind of equality of which I speak is simply the mutual awareness of and respect that acknowledges you are both of equal value before the Lord: "There is neither Jew nor Greek, there is neither slave nor free, there is neither male nor female; for you are all one in Christ Jesus" (Galatians 3:28).

I maintain that we are called to different, complementary roles: men to headship and women to partnership. This calling will likely vary in different couples. In one, the wife may be the primary breadwinner while the husband stays home with the children. In another, the wife works so the husband can finish his degree. In yet another, the husband works two jobs so his wife can be home full-time with their small children. On and on the variations within each couple. Based on individual strengths and weaknesses, gifts and talents, the division of roles and responsibilities can be distributed so each partner's contribution complements the other's for maximum effect.

But what about the biblical roles of husband and wife? What does it mean that the man is appointed head of the marriage? What does it mean for husbands and wives to relate like Christ and the church? What does it truly mean to be submissive? Much controversy often swirls around the biblical instruction regarding the roles of husbands and wives, headship and submission. I'm afraid that too often God's Word has been taken out of context and misused to suppress women and keep them from reaching their full potential. If we examine Scripture and truly seek to understand the comparison between husband and wives and Christ and the church, I believe we realize that the relationship is based on mutual submission and interactive support. Let's consider the way Paul explains the dynamic of this relationship in one of his letters to the early church.

> Wives, submit to your own husbands, as to the Lord. For the husband is head of the wife, as also Christ is head of the church; and He is the Savior of the body. Therefore, just as the church is subject to Christ, so let the wives be to their own husbands in everything.
>
> Husbands, love your wives, just as Christ also loved the church and gave Himself for her, that He might sanctify and cleanse her with the washing of water by the word, that He might present her to Himself a glorious church, not having spot or wrinkle or any such thing, but that she should be holy and without blemish. So husbands ought to love their own wives as their own bodies; he who loves his wife loves himself . . .
>
> This is a great mystery, but I speak concerning Christ and the church. Nevertheless let each one of you in particular so love his own wife as himself, and let the wife see that she respects her husband. (Ephesians 5:22–33)

There's a lot to reflect upon here. Many ladies tell me they are uncomfortable with this passage because it asks them to do something they can't always do: submit to their husbands.

They are afraid it means they must do everything their husband tells them to do, that they won't be allowed to think and choose for themselves. But this passage is more complex than simply exhorting men to lead and women to follow. No, I believe it has something to do with how we are made in our Creator's image as women and men and how we are to pursue oneness in marriage. We are designed to complete and complement one another so that we fulfill our marriage vows. And just as it takes two to make the marriage work, Paul's instruction here is based on complementary dynamics: a wife's submission complements her husband's leadership; a wife's obedience to her husband in everything is in response to her husband's sacrificial love; loving each other is a reflection of loving oneself.

I don't believe this passage informs us to be doormats or wallflowers and do everything our husbands ask of us. Nor do I believe it is meant to be applied literally to all roles within a relationship. So much of a marriage's success is based on the *attitude* of each partner in viewing his or her contribution to the union. If a man is not following God and living by His principles, it is awfully hard for a woman to want to walk alongside him. However, when a man is in touch with the power of the Holy Spirit living within him, and he earnestly seeks to fulfill the calling the Lord places on him and his family, I believe his wife will be compelled to walk alongside him. She may be scared, uncertain, nervous, and anxious, but she'll have peace in her man's decisions—choices made together as a team—about how to fulfill their calling. She will experience a confidence that is supernatural, not based on how smart her man is or how kind, not on how much money he makes or the kind of car he drives.

And men need this kind of support, which can come from

only their helpmeet. Yes, it's certainly important for you to believe in your husband's abilities and talents. He needs to know you think he's the smartest, greatest, best-looking man in the city (most of the time). But it takes more than just a strong couple united in their attraction to one another. It takes a shared faith built on a joint calling from our Lord to provide the undergirding that will see you through the hard times—the days when tempers are short and bills are overdue, through sleepless nights when the children are sick or harsh words have been spoken.

Those are the moments when it's difficult to trust him and submit to what it means to be a wife. Most of us have suffered through those times more than we'd like. But those are also the moments when he's suffering as well. Dear lady, your husband is charged with loving you as he loves his own body, with making you clean and spotless like Jesus Christ redeeming His church. Basically, a man is charged with covering his wife, serving as a blanket of security, love, and protection, not a scratchy, suffocating cloak of manipulation.

It may be challenging, my sister, to allow yourself to rest in his covering, especially if you're the one in the public spotlight. You may be so used to leading in the boardroom or performing on the platform that you struggle to let down in the home. But if you don't allow yourself to rest in his strength and headship, then you will find yourself exhausted from defending yourself all the time. You may not need him to earn a paycheck, to fight off wild animals and other dangers, but you do need him to believe you are worth fighting for. Once an understanding of this kind of covering is in place, the marriage can bend to endure many of the hardships of life without breaking.

Completion Not Competition

Men and women often negotiate the dance of their roles within the relationship with more freedom today. Our society is more equitable in its appreciation of women's gifts and supportive of men's creativity, artistry, and domestic talents. However, with this new freedom also comes a not-so-subtle danger. Instead of trying to complement one another, the couple begins to compete with one another. Suddenly, she's making more money so he feels threatened, especially if she likes having this kind of power over her man. Or perhaps he's going back to college and becoming involved in a world very different from hers with her high school education. No doubt, it can be threatening.

This is the time you must stay connected to one another. You must make the time, no matter how late he must wait up on you or how early you must awake to see him before work. As you find yourself drifting apart during certain seasons, it takes special effort to solidify the bond between you. This is where you must remember that you are both of equal worth, both valuable beyond compare. It's not a matter of competition. You shouldn't need to prove yourself to him nor he to you. Your relationship should be the safe harbor where the cares and stress melt away, not where they're compounded into a wedge between the two of you.

Avoiding competition will also mean maintaining priorities. Leave your work at the office and build a hedge around your home as a place of family, rest, and security. Beware of coworkers, and even friends, who may encourage a competitive mindset. Perhaps it's a disapproving comment about your husband's origins at the company dinner party. Maybe it's your own insecurity about what his friends think of your intelligence. When you hear someone either directly or indirectly disparage your spouse, you must weed it out right then. Politely tell the speaker you don't appreciate their mistaken perceptions, and then move on. If you allow these voices to play on your insecurities, the social or educational fracture between you and your husband will become an earthquake. Guard your marriage and contribute to your teammate. When tempted to compete or focus on your own accomplishments, remember that you share the same goals.

Also, to avoid the pitfalls of competition, please realize, dear sister, that part of sharing equal billing is sharing equal sacrifice and responsibility. Often it's difficult to let go of your idealistic notions that life will go smoothly as long as you both love each other. It won't. Hard times come when he loses his job, when you take a second job to help pay his school loans, when you're pregnant and suffering from high blood pressure, when you're forced to move cross-country to care for aging parents. Then it takes a shared vision and a renewed commitment to where you're going as a couple, what you both invest in as your dream, the ways your individual callings have been interwoven together into a cord stronger than its separate threads.

The nuts and bolts of this complementary support will take some trial and error. When a couple are first getting started, often after the first blush of romance begins to grow into the new bloom of real love, these issues must be discussed and experimented with. Maybe you don't cook well, but your man does. Perhaps you have a gift for finances and making money, and your husband is more creative and artistic. Or (something I have heard from many women lately) perhaps you long to stay at home with your children but don't want to be perceived by your female executive-type friends as less than them—as old-fashioned because you want to create and organize your house as a home or because you want to be present for your baby's first words or initial steps.

These are areas you and your spouse must discuss, preferably before your marriage, or at least during the early stages. And there are some things to keep in mind in dealing with your gentleman in this area. No matter how progressive the two of you may be in your thinking, no matter how intelligent, open-minded, and supportive the two of you may be, you will still have to deal with some issues of gender related to identity and some issues of gender related to your culture.

Most men want to provide for their women and their families. It may sound outdated, sexist, even barbaric, but the male ego needs to feel that he can provide and protect those he loves. So if you're making more money than him or supporting him while he's in school or in a lower-paying career, you need to address this head-on. Ask him how he feels about it. Better yet, share your concerns or fears. He may be just fine with it (and if he's too comfortable letting you support him, then that's another problem!) or he may not even realize that he cares what other people might think. The key is in keeping lines of communication open and two sided.

Advanced Communication

Go into any bookstore and you will find several shelves devoted to improving communication between marriage partners. You will see books on how to speak a man's love language, how to understand his differences, and even books on how to know what planet he's from! Many of these are excellent. There is much to be said about understanding that your husband is different from you, that he receives and appreciates love in different ways than you do, and that it helps if you understand where each other is coming from. Without making specific endorsements, I encourage you to do some homework and seek out works to address particular areas of struggle. Having said that, however, let me offer a few suggestions of my own about how to best communicate with your man.

Know each other's unspoken language. Can you recall a time when you were at a party, bored by the tedious inquiries of strangers, trapped by the web of small talk with the hostess? Most of us seek to avoid such affairs, but often they're unavoidable due to work and civic affiliations. Suddenly your spouse appears at your side, makes an appropriate excuse, and leads you to the door for a quick exit. He's your hero, not just for getting you out of an awkward situation, but because he read your body language from across the room. Or perhaps you can recall a conversation you and your husband had with a third party that required diplomacy. Even as words were exchanged among the three of you, you and your spouse carried on a silent conversation with your eyes alone.

Such is the magic of knowing and loving someone intimately. I encourage you to study your spouse's response to various situations. Learn when to stop him before he says too much. Know how to draw him out when he needs to say more. Develop code words that allow you to rescue each other from awkward social situations. This is one of the gifts of communicating with your spouse.

Timing really is everything. However, such in-tune conversations often make it that much harder when language becomes inadequate and emotions get in the way of expressing what needs to be said. When you talk, be sensitive to his days, his moods, his needs, just as you want him to be aware of yours. During the hectic times when one or both of you are working, traveling, or shuffling kids back and forth between the orthodontist and piano lessons and football practice, it's essential that you make time together a priority. Make a date night or other quiet time a part of each week's schedule so you have time to talk about your concerns and stay connected with each other's heart. Keep in touch throughout the day, even if for just a few minutes on the phone to hear the sound of each other's voice.

Love is the universal language. As I mentioned, much has been written and studied about the different ways men and women communicate. Generally speaking, you must realize that when you discuss things, the man is usually reading on the surface, listening for information. Conversely, most ladies I know—and this is true for myself as well—do not listen so much for information as they seek to hear the tone and emotional content. We're listening with our hearts as much as our ears. We often want to connect through our emotions while he often wants to correspond by voice.

It sounds stereotypical, but many ladies can use this difference to help their men get in touch with and stay connected to what the men are feeling. And many husbands can provide a more objective perspective for their wives and help them to not take everything personally. Once again, the notion of complementary balance comes to mind. When you have different communication styles, especially when discussing conflict, you must remember that love is a universal language.

Our words have great power to harm others and to heal others. The Proverbs record, "Death and life are in the power of the tongue, and those who love it will eat its fruit" (18:21). James goes so far as to state, "Even so the tongue is a little member and boasts great things. See how great a forest a little fire kindles!" (3:5). Learn to share your heart but hold your tongue when angry. If you base your language in love, you can persevere and learn to develop a shared alphabet.

Speak quietly into the silence. As a communicator, you must learn how to speak softly into the deadly silence that comes in certain seasons. It can be the silence that comes from a routine leading to boredom in the relationship. You both say and do the same things day after day rather than engaging with and in each other's interior world, which is never boring. Or the silence emerges from the tragic losses of life. When his position is downsized unexpectedly at the company, when his brother succumbs to cancer, when his child lies in a hospital operating room, he will be afraid, perhaps even unable, to articulate the crippling terror invading his soul. If you're like me, you will want to talk, to allow him to share his feelings and thoughts, to get it out. But he will be holding it all in, screaming in his withdrawn silence and sorrow.

How do you speak when his soul screams in silence? I don't have a "right" answer, but I'll never forget when my husband's mother passed away. As I said earlier, she was a wonderful lady and was like a mother to me as well. My love for her ran deep, and certainly I felt an incredible loss at her passing. But, oh, the loss my husband suffered. It was raw and painful and sent him into depths of himself he had never before experienced. His faith was tested by the searing pain of grief. He would be calm and in control one moment and upset with tears in his eyes the next. He told me repeatedly that he didn't know what to say to me, to anyone.

I had never seen him like this. I wasn't sure how to speak into his loss, but I knew I had to try. Some days I said too much or brought up memories that were excruciatingly painful. Yet into his deadly silence, I tried to offer a quiet, safe place for him to feel and share his pain.

Every time you confront deadly silence will require unique and special care. There's a fine line here, and you will have to find your own way in its boundaries. On one hand, he needs you now more than ever. He needs to feel loved and secure, with a new anchor point in your relationship now that another fixture has been stripped away. Accept this need from him and make your heart available without demanding that he talk and explain his feelings. In most cases, you may safely assume his heart is wounded and his soul is bleeding. Be there for him so when he is ready to talk or needs to express his hurt out loud, you are available to share his pain. Don't expect him to handle it the way you would handle it, or the way the other men in your life—your father, brothers, or old boyfriends—have handled it. The pain is his and his alone until he's willing to share it. Speak softly into his silence, and his heart will respond in due time.

Growing Pains

As we seek to support and walk alongside our man, we will be challenged by many obstacles. And I know that even if we try to anticipate the blows of life, they still take us by surprise with their intensity or severity. That's why we must build our marriage upon the firm rock of our faith in the Lord. Jesus said,

"The rain came down, the streams rose, and the winds blew and beat against that house; yet it did not fall, because it had its foundation on the rock" (Matthew 7:25 NIV). The rains will fall on you. So let your husband cover you. The streams will rise. So run alongside each other, instead of one racing ahead, to seek shelter together. The winds will come and beat against your house. So speak words of love, forgiveness, and grace that will endure like a solid cornerstone. This is how to transform the storms of life into growing pains for dimensions of oneness. This is how you strive together to share equal billing and grow together so you are each more than you could have ever been alone. As you pray for your husband and the type of relational house the two of you are building together, consider the following prayer as a way of voicing your heart's desire for truly sharing a life together.

―――――――――――――― ⌒ ――――――――――――――

Dear Giver of All Good Gifts, I'm so thankful for the many blessings You've bestowed upon me, especially for this wonderful man in my life. I ask that as we face life's challenges, the losses and trials that inevitably come from living in a fallen world, we would grow together and not apart. Allow us to turn to You and to each other for comfort and protection, for shelter from these storms of life. May we serve each other in mutual submission, in selfless love, and with contagious joy. Allow our partnership to reflect the love present between Jesus and His bride, the Church. Keep our hearts strong and our spirits light. Amen.

―――――――――――――― ⌒ ――――――――――――――

Questions and Suggestions

1. How would you describe your experience sharing the spotlight with your man? What unique challenges have you overcome? Which ones remain obstacles to ongoing growth in your relationship?

2. Whose career has seemed to take precedent in your marriage? How have the two of you delegated responsibilities? How do you feel about the dynamics of your arrangement?

3. Make a short list of ways to serve your husband this week. Choose one item and serve him with gladness. It may be something as mundane as picking up his dry cleaning or preparing his favorite meal. Or it may be more creative, such as arranging a surprise boys' night out or watching his favorite sporting event with him.

4. In your journal, write out the delegation of chores and responsibilities that would best suit both your giftedness and your husband's. Now compare this ideal delegation list to the way your household and marriage currently operate. Note the discrepancies and then plan a time to go over your findings with your husband. Try to be non-defensive, objective, and sincere in reconsidering the division of labor and roles in your home.

5. How has your faith, both as individuals and as a couple, helped you endure some of the storms of life during your marriage? How could your faith as a couple become even stronger?

10

Marriage in the Middle:
Juggling Life on a Tightrope

She's up before the rest of the house, showering and dressing, packing kids' lunches while putting on makeup. She checks e-mail and finishes a report for her ten o'clock board meeting while helping her husband find a pair of dress socks that match. She drops the kids off at school, stops to get the oil changed on the car, then picks up pastries for her meeting at work. She leads the meeting with a confidence and poise that impresses everyone present. She works through lunch, eating a leftover éclair, then realizes she's late to pick up her daughter for an orthodontist's appointment. She shuttles back and forth, taking her cell phone with her to stay linked to the office and to her mother, who suffers from Alzheimer's in a medical care facility across town. By six o'clock she's assessing what's left on her desk and planning the next day. Her husband's making dinner for the kids, and she's meeting them at the church at seven for the week's revival service.

Whew! It makes me dizzy just to describe such a day, let alone recall the ones when my own life seems this out of control. Perhaps you're not juggling the same balls in the air, but

I'm guessing that if you've reached the beginning of the middle of life, you know what I'm talking about. There never seem to be enough hours in the day. You're in the midst of pursuing your life's calling, as a supportive wife, perhaps as a mother or caretaker for children, and as a maker and sustainer of the home. Add in some other variables—a career, for instance, or your own home business or even volunteer work for your church—and suddenly the merry-go-round is whirling faster.

Then some seasons bring their own set of complications and concerns: needs of the children for doctor's appointments, music lessons, and sports practice. You may find yourself caretaker of an ailing parent or an in-law as their health declines. Your job or your husband's may require extended travel in order for you to succeed and reach the next level. You may have thought you were ready for retirement when suddenly you're raising your grandchildren. Life can certainly throw curveballs into your juggling act and upend the best-laid plans.

In these seasons, when it feels as if you're not only juggling too many balls in the air but you're forced to walk a tightrope high above the net as you do so, you must learn to ground yourself in your primary relationship: your marriage. It's easy when you're younger and just arriving in this busy midlife season to think, *I'll never take my husband for granted. I'll never get so busy that I won't take good care of myself. I'm capable of staying balanced and maintaining my priorities.* But then life happens, and you find yourself caught up in the white-water rapids of other people's needs, and it seems you're capsizing for the final time. This is when you must maintain the secure raft of your partnership if you're going to navigate and pass safely through the churning waters. One of the major leaks that often springs in this life-giving raft of marriage is what I call the myth of "having it all." Please allow me to elaborate.

The Myth of Having It All

In her very short story "Girl," author Jamaica Kincaid presents a young woman remembering the litany of advice her mother gave her while growing up. "Don't walk barehead in the hot sun," her mother told her, and "This is how to make a bread pudding." The instructions include the right way to iron, bake, bathe, plant okra, set a table, and tell if bread is fresh. Although the story is only a page long, the advice becomes overwhelming. It's humorous and poignant, for I think most of us can recall our mamas giving us similar advice, and if not our mamas, then surely the ladies who helped us grow up.

When we consider all the messages that accompany us into our present juggling phase of life, it's no wonder we can end up confused and overwhelmed. On one hand, many of us look at the traditional roles our mothers and grandmothers filled— the way they worked at home, raised the kids, and submitted to our fathers and grandfathers, often based on force and tradition and not on love or respect. We may have quickly decided this was not the kind of life we wanted for ourselves. Perhaps our mothers even spoke their dreams of a better life into our hearts. Out of their struggles, the past generations of women worked hard to make a better way for their daughters so we would have more opportunities—for education, for independence, for careers and economic advantages. We were not forced to suppress our intelligence or our giftedness, and settle for a life of domestic chores and subservience, as so many women did.

However, for later generations of women, including my own, the pendulum may have swung to the other extreme. Our mothers' message of hope was transformed into the mantra of endless possibility and limitless pressure. We were expected to be Wonder Women with college degrees, a successful husband, beautiful children, and a business of our own, even as we cooked, cleaned, and decorated more often than Martha Stewart and Oprah combined. It makes me tired just thinking about all a twenty-first-century woman is supposed to do!

I'm certainly not complaining about having too many opportunities. No, dear sister, I am most grateful for the changes in our culture and society even in my own lifetime. I have seen tremendous change in the status of women and the numerous opportunities that have opened up to us. We have come a long way, and we're not through with our journey.

The problem I'm talking about with mixed messages doesn't have to do with having more opportunities. This expanded horizon for women is certainly God's gift in breaking cultural barriers of pride, fear, and prejudice. No, the problem comes when we feel the need to fulfill every opportunity, saying yes to everything that comes our way instead of saying yes to our calling along the way. We think we must juggle every ball that gets thrown in our path instead of choosing only a few balls to juggle well.

How do we decide which ones to juggle and which ones to let fall? That's a question we must constantly ask ourselves and present before the Lord. I also believe we must constantly remind ourselves that even though the possibilities are endless, we are not! We are finite, human creatures with limits—physical limits and limits of time and resources. We simply cannot do everything. Nor are we called to. The good news about expanded possibilities is that we can now pursue all we are called to. We don't have to give up our dream of being an astronaut or a doctor or the CEO of a Fortune 500 company simply because we're women. Nor do we need to be ashamed of wanting to be a good mother and homemaker.

I believe we must realize that most phases of our lives mark distinct seasons. Scripture often reminds us that we experience different seasons in our lives, and throughout them all we are to seek the Lord. The writer of Ecclesiastes reminds us of the ever-changing nature of life in a beautiful, and perhaps familiar, poem:

> To everything there is a season,
> A time for every purpose under heaven:
> A time to be born,
> And a time to die;
> A time to plant,
> And a time to pluck what is planted;
> A time to kill,
> And a time to heal;
> A time to break down,
> And a time to build up;
> A time to weep,
> And a time to laugh;
> A time to mourn,
> And a time to dance;
> A time to cast away stones,
> And a time to gather stones;
> A time to embrace,
> And a time to refrain from embracing;
> A time to gain,
> And a time to lose;
> A time to keep,
> And a time to throw away;

A time to tear,
And a time to sew;
A time to keep silence,
And a time to speak;
A time to love,
And a time to hate;
A time of war,
And a time of peace. (Ecclesiastes 3:1–8)

Can you identify your present season of life from these categories? Certainly we can experience a peaceful season at home even as disagreements and political infighting create a season of war at work; this may only complicate our choices and the various items in our juggling act. Then again, sometimes our life seasons will converge, and all areas will seem to be working in one accord. However, most of the time, I believe it's unrealistic to expect to have a perfect season of bliss where everything goes your way. This feeds into the myth of having it all and being a superwoman with no weaknesses and no areas of need herself.

Instead of trying to have it all at once or be everything to everybody, we must focus on the basics of our lives: who we are and what matters most in our present season. Unfortunately, this runs counter to our culture. Advertisers and the entertainment industry would have us believe women should always look stunning as they command the office, nurture their children, encourage their husbands, complete their housework, and teach Sunday school at church. I'm afraid we can't have it all, at least not all at once.

I encourage you to recognize and respect the season of life in which you are presently planted. This may mean putting some dreams on hold temporarily while you help pay the bills.

It may mean accepting a season of grief as you mourn the loss of someone dear to you. It could mean embracing the craziness that comes with mothering small children or the concern that lingers as your babies grow up. However, regardless of the season of life you are called to acknowledge and embrace, know that some aspects of your life remain constant. You may not be able to have it all, as our culture often wishes us to believe, but you can have peace in the midst of all that swirls around you. Let's consider how this can be accomplished by looking at one of the most extraordinary women described in all of Scripture.

Wonder Woman

In Proverbs 31, which may be familiar to you, we find an unparalleled description of an extraordinary woman. She's a virtuous wife, an industrious entrepreneur, a thrifty manager, and a godly mother to her children. She's beloved by her maidservants, the poor, and those in need. How does she do it? Perhaps she may seem even more intimidating as a role model than Wonder Woman! Yet if we examine each of her qualities and see how she walks her life's tightrope, I believe we'll see that we have the same resources available to us.

> Who can find a virtuous wife?
> For her worth is far above rubies.
> The heart of her husband safely trusts her;
> So he will have no lack of gain.
> She does him good and not evil
> All the days of her life. (Proverbs 31:10–12)

It seems striking to me that this description of our Wonder Woman is grounded not in her abilities but in her character.

She is virtuous, valuable, trustworthy, and righteous. So often when we're overwhelmed by life we forget who we are. Ladies often tell me they feel so exhausted and fragmented by all the demands on them, they don't know if they're going or coming. But we must remember our starting place and our reliance on the Lord. Indeed, this passage returns to this notion: "Charm is deceitful and beauty is passing, but a woman who fears the Lord, she shall be praised" (Proverbs 31:30).

We must go beyond appearances, dear sister. The externals are deceitful. Women, especially Christian women, work so hard to appear to have it all together—to always look just right, present the kids well dressed and well behaved, have all the appointments scheduled neatly in a row, and coordinate an exciting career. But usually we're trying to focus only on the outside because we're tired, afraid, and overwhelmed on the inside. We must not ignore those feelings. Instead, we must use them to draw closer to God, to remember who we are as His precious daughters, and to become who He has created us to be, not who we think everyone else wants us to be. If we depend on Him, we find new resources from which we can accomplish many things. We see this as the description of our biblical Wonder Woman continues:

> She seeks wool and flax,
> And willingly works with her hands.
> She is like the merchant ships,
> She brings her food from afar.
> She also rises while it is yet night,
> And provides food for her household,
> And a portion for her maidservants.
> She considers a field and buys it;
> From her profits she plants a vineyard.

She girds herself with strength,
And strengthens her arms. (Proverbs 31:13–17)

Perhaps you're thinking to yourself, *I'm not a crafty-creative-type woman; this doesn't really apply to me.* Or maybe, *I'm not a businesswoman so I'm not sure what there is for me in this passage.* Granted, we may not all be knitters and have an eye for real estate investment, but we are called to be life-givers. Whether it's working with our hands or providing food for our households or reinvesting profit from one endeavor in another, we must be willing to nurture, to give, and to birth new ventures. We must know who we are so we can be comfortable giving freely of ourselves and our talents.

So often in our me-first culture, we're afraid that if we give all we've got to those around us, we'll lose ourselves and our identity. And that's a very real danger. We must maintain healthy boundaries and take care of ourselves (we'll address this in the next chapter). However, there's something positive to be said for giving yourself away, for using your talents and abilities to their fullest, in order to find yourself. Jesus says, "He who finds his life will lose it, and he who loses his life for My sake will find it" (Matthew 10:39). You may be surprised sometimes when you're feeling overwhelmed that the antidote is to loosen your grip and consider what you're holding back out of fear and insecurity. The Lord may be calling you to risk new ventures and seek out His opportunities. This certainly seems to be part of the strategy of this woman in Proverbs 31:

She is not afraid of snow for her household,
For all her household is clothed with scarlet.
She makes tapestry for herself;
Her clothing is fine linen and purple . . .

Strength and honor are her clothing;
She shall rejoice in time to come. (21–22, 25)

Do you notice something special about this passage? There are numerous references to clothing and colors that were usually reserved for royalty at the time: scarlet and purple, linen and tapestry. It's as if this woman is a queen and her royal household is draped with bright colors befitting the appropriate splendor. However, our woman in this passage is not above spinning the cloth herself. She is humble and hardworking. It's unlikely that any actual queen would do the clothmaking and weaving herself; she would have her servants do it for her. But this woman seems to have class, character, and dignity, and yet she is not above hard work and self-sacrifice. She's a catcher of beauty for herself and for those around her. She not only clothes herself in beautiful garments but covers her household in the royal colors as well. The writer seems to reinforce the source of her power in the conclusion of the passage: "Strength and honor are her clothing; she shall rejoice in time to come" (v. 25). It's as if he's making sure we understand her *character traits*, not her fine clothes, elevate her to the status of royalty. They simply reflect who she is inside.

I believe we are called to the same balance in our character as well. We should strive for the best and enjoy the privileges of being God's royal children. However, we should not falsely elevate ourselves above others and become conceited or arrogant. This concept can be hard to balance in seasons of overwhelming busyness. We may be tempted to have a pity party because we've lost sight of our true identity or our vital priorities. However, if we clothe ourselves in strength and honor, we will be able to rejoice, just as the woman in Proverbs. Perhaps this is part of the reason she is truly blessed:

> Her children rise up and call her blessed;
> Her husband also, and he praises her:
> "Many daughters have done well,
> But you excel them all."
> Charm is deceitful and beauty is passing,
> But a woman who fears the LORD,
> she shall be praised.
> Give her of the fruit of her hands,
> And let her own works praise her in the gates.
>   (Proverbs 31:28–31)

The description concludes by emphasizing where it began: The character of this woman is what makes her great. Her children and husband praise her because of who she is and where she is in her relationship with the Lord. She reaps what she sows as the fruit of her labors speak louder than any words ever could.

What will the fruit of your hands say about you, dear lady? What would your family and friends say about you if you were suddenly called home by the Father? Please forgive me if this sounds morbid; that is not my intention. But I believe it can be extremely helpful in focusing your priorities to consider the consequences of your investments. What have you sown into the character of your children? How will your husband know you have loved him? What will your legacy be to future generations?

This is where we must consider that most of our choices are not between bad and good but between good and better. Please let me explain why this is so crucial to maintaining balance in our lives in the midst of the juggling-on-a-tightrope kinds of seasons.

Pruning the Branches

I don't have much of a green thumb, but I love the beauty of a well-kept garden. And I've gardened enough to know such beauty doesn't happen by accident. I'll never forget a small cottonwood tree we had in our yard. It shot up with what appeared to be several strong, trunklike branches emanating from its base. However, when the "tree doctor" came by a few weeks later to assess some nearby shrubbery, he commented that we should cut back all but one of those branches. When I asked him why, since the tree seemed to be flourishing so well as it was, he said, "Because if you don't, the tree will die. It will grow like wildfire for a while, but then it will not be able to support itself because so much of its energy is spread too thin. For a tree to flourish, you need one main trunk with strong, selective branches. If you don't prune this one, it will grow uncontained until it dies."

I took his words to heart, and I encourage you to do the same. As oversimplified as it sounds, you must make your marriage, your home, and your family your "trunk." Your tree must have its roots in your dependence on God and your nourishment from His Word. He will sustain you with rich nutrients, water, and sunshine. And you must prune the branches that are not contributing to the overall health of your trunk and its production of fruit. Jesus reminds us that this principle is one the Father Himself uses to enable us to fulfill our full potential: "Every branch in Me that does not bear fruit

He takes away; and every branch that bears fruit He prunes, that it may bear more fruit" (John 15:2).

But how do you know which branches to keep and which to prune? As I mentioned before, this is a crucial question. It will require hard decisions in which you must choose among some wonderful options. That's why it's so important to realize the seeming possibility of choosing all of them and succeeding in the wild juggling act that ensues is nothing more than an illusion, that myth of "having it all." Instead, part of the way to go about pruning your life is to get honest with yourself about what you love and why you love it. Another part is to seek the counsel of your husband and honor his opinions about what is best for you as a couple and the family as a whole.

This will likely involve learning to say no to things that really do not further your peace, your family's peace, or your walk with the Lord. Learn to choose between good and better because that's where the battle lies; those are the times you find yourself picking up more balls to juggle. Learn to say a polite and firm "No" as often as needed in order to protect what matters most. Don't be afraid to disappoint other people—it's inevitable. Remember that when you say no to a good invitation, opportunity, or possibility, you are also saying yes to a better one: honoring your main priorities, pursuing peace, and focusing on those you love most.

As you seek to discern how to strike balance between good and better choices, don't overlook the power of prayer to keep you focused and attuned to God's voice in your life. If we but listen, He often speaks to our hearts and instructs us on our journey down His path. As the demands of others spin out of control and begin to crash in on us, we can draw strength from His promise to us: "Be strong and of good courage, do not fear nor be afraid of them; for the LORD your God, He is the One who goes with you. He will not leave you nor forsake you" (Deuteronomy 31:6).

Finally, in order to survive the necessary juggling act on the tightrope of the middle years of life, you must learn to take good care of yourself. What does such self-care look like amid the office reports, soccer practices, and grocery shopping? How can taking care of yourself actually enable you to offer greater support to the men in your life? In order to explore these questions, take a deep breath, find a quiet moment in your favorite chair with a cup of coffee, and consider using the following prayer as a means of catching your spiritual breath and assessing how to prune and simplify your present load.

Dear Keeper of My Soul, I pause now for these minutes in Your presence. I pray You would sustain me as I seek to do more than I could ever do on my own. Please help me to know how my gifts are best used. Enable me to discern between good choices and Your choices. Allow me to see with Your eyes so I might know what to let go of and what to carry forward. Give me stamina and wisdom, patience and peace. Allow me to focus my priorities on what You value most and to love the man You have placed in my life. Protect our marriage, and help me to value it as much as You do. Amen.

Questions and Suggestions

1. How would you describe your present season of life? What are the specific and unique demands on your time and energy? How are you managing to juggle them all?

2. Which demands do you wish you could drop from your juggling act? What keeps you from dropping them?

3. What intimidates you most about the Proverbs 31 Wonder Woman? In what ways does she inspire or encourage you? What would it require for you to become more like her while remaining true to yourself and your own unique calling?

4. For one week in your journal record how your time is spent. Note every errand, shopping trip, soccer practice, school concert, church small group, and work meeting. Choose one item from your list that, while a good endeavor, is not the best use of your time and energy during your present season. Eliminate this item from your list with no guilt whatsoever. Remember that saying no to this item means saying yes to your priorities.

5. Recall some times in your life when you've been forced to recognize your limitations. What can you learn from these times about taking better care of yourself? I encourage you this week to go on a prayer walk and enjoy the beauty of God's creation as you discuss with Him how to pursue peace and balance in your life.

11

Finding "Me-Time":
Self-Care Without Self-Absorption

Imagine lying on a soft chaise lounge, your body warmed by the shining sun that graces a sky so blue, you can't tell where the water meets the horizon. A cool breeze softens the tropical heat along with the cool drink beside you. Waves lap near your feet, gently nibbling away at the sand. You don't know what time it is, and you don't care. No one is there to disturb you.

Blue-sky moments like this can be as rare as they are worshipful. You may even have difficulty imagining yourself in such a setting. If that's the case, and you struggle with the whole notion of making time for yourself to rest, you may need it now more than ever.

As we discussed in the last chapter, we must learn to take care of ourselves if we are to survive the juggling, tightrope-walking seasons of life. Perhaps you hear this so often that it has lost its meaning. However, I cannot emphasize enough that if you're not willing to rest, to pursue balance in your life, and to take good care of your own needs, you will not make it through the storms of life. You will not have anything left to give your husband as he depletes his own resources and looks to you for comfort or support. You will not be able to care for ailing parents or needy children or precious grandchildren. You will lose your creativity and vision for success in your business endeavors. If you don't make me-time a priority on your schedule, then you risk burning yourself into a parched desert of despair.

This may be the hardest truth to convey to many of the women I meet. Many ladies tell me they feel as if they need permission to take care of themselves. They feel guilty and self-indulgent if they take a nap in the afternoon, schedule a massage, or plan lunch with a girlfriend. They say they're spending time that could be used more efficiently in the office or at home or at church. And they say they're spending money that could be spent on other items or needs.

Certainly, there's a balance; I don't want you to think I'm encouraging you to justify your behavior every time you want to get away or splurge on a new pair of shoes. But most of the women I see, especially Christian women, tend to play the martyr easier than they play the diva. Many of them know they're burning out but they don't know how to rekindle the warmth and illumination from their priority passions.

My guess is that the last chapter had you nodding your head in agreement and wondering how much more you can take before you reach a breaking point. It reminds me of a valuable lesson I learned when I first started college. In my freshman English class, our professor was an older woman with a passion for excellence in communication and a motherly attitude toward her students. She allowed us three absences for the entire semester and made it clear that after that time there would be no exceptions.

For various reasons, I missed my three classes and then received an invitation for a weekend trip home with one of my girlfriends. However, she was leaving early, and I would be forced to miss my class. When I went to my professor and asked for her permission, she said, "Serita, you're a good student, and I understand about wanting to go with your friend. However, you've made a commitment, not just to me, but to yourself to do your best in this class, and I'm afraid that needs to come first in this choice. You may miss class and still pass. But you'll be letting yourself down because you'll have missed part of your education. Each day brings its own wisdom." At first I thought she was merely trying to lay a guilt trip on me, but then I thought about what she was saying. I had never considered what I would be risking if I missed the class. It seemed easily justified in the moment, but put in the perspective of my entire education, I realized I was cheating myself out of my reason for being there.

What does this have to do with your need to take care of yourself? Everything! If you keep putting off that exercise program, that dance class, those morning walks and weekend getaways, you're cheating yourself out of your priority. *But, Serita*, you're thinking, *I can't fit it into my schedule. I'm too tired to exercise or even relax! The kids have too many appointments and sports practices. My husband needs me to help out with his business. My parents need me to take care of them. The church counts on me to help prepare for Sunday services. I feel selfish turning down their requests just so I can go lounge around or take a vacation.*

I hear you. And I know all the reasons and excuses for not allowing me-time. However, I'm convinced that if you don't strike a balance between your legitimate needs and the present demands on your being, you will one day be forced to consider it.

Illness or physical injury, divorce or loss of employment, depression or burnout will sap your spirit and claim you as a casualty.

With this in mind, my first piece of advice to break through this kind of "I can't take the time to focus on me" attitude is to avoid either/or thinking. *Either I remain a responsible wife, mother, daughter, employee, church worker, friend, etc., we so often think, or I become a self-absorbed, spoiled creature of comfort.* Not true! Try to avoid this extreme mind-set and replace it with the message: "I'm able to be a better wife, mother, daughter, employee, etc., because I take good care of myself each day."

One of my dearest friends learned this message the hard way, but at least she finally learned it. She became so burned out and depressed for several months that she finally visited a doctor who tried her on various antidepressant medications. Each drug seemed to have worse side effects than the one before it. Finally, the doctor shared with her that a lot of research supported that aerobic exercise could be as, or more, effective than drugs in treating depression than drug therapy. At her doctor's suggestion, my friend began to walk each morning. After a month, she began to jog. Soon she found herself running five to six times a week. She loved it.

"I'll never be fast or what you typically think of as an athlete," she tells me, "but I do this for me." Soon she hopes to train for her first marathon! When I asked her about the amount of time her exercise has taken, she said, "It's nothing compared to how much time I was losing in misspent energy and sleepless nights. I'm much more productive and balanced because I take care of my needs before I try to take care of everyone else's."

Wise words, indeed, dear lady. Whether it's exercise you need or time to stare out the window so you can pray and reflect on your life, you must slow down and reprioritize your time. If you don't, you will not be able to give your real gifts to those you love the most.

Cleaning Our Closets

If you feel guilty or self-indulgent for taking time away, it may be hard at first. Please realize, however, that you are being much more selfish if you insist on running yourself ragged so everyone will think you're tireless, selfless, and perpetually busy. If you do not set hedges around your own needs and the needs of your husband and family, then you will be consumed by other people's needs and other people's willingness to exploit you. Requests for your time and energy will come from work, from the neighborhood, and from church: to volunteer to tutor kids after school, help out with the church kitchen, organize the company retreat, write the grant for the government funds. Perhaps you will feel called to some of these. But please do not try to do it all. As we noted in the last chapter, the myth of having and doing it all is just that—a myth.

Instead, you must remain vigilant about pursuing only your true passions. This may involve going over your schedule for the next few months or even the rest of this year and prioritizing every item that has a bite of your time. I'm guessing they're all important, worthwhile, necessary commitments and appointments. However, I'm also confident not all of them reflect your passionate priorities. Pray over these items, perhaps even rank them from one to five or have your spouse or your best friend help you. Then bow out of those lower-ranking items. They are the items you must reluctantly release, no matter how nice it would be to fulfill them.

It's funny, too, that often we need an outside opinion—one that's more objective than our own. It reminds me of cleaning out our closets at home. Recently, my oldest daughter and I agreed to help one another go through our closets and remove all the garments we no longer wore so we could pass them on to others in need. As I began to sort through her jeans and blouses, her dresses and sweaters, I held up item after item that I hadn't seen her wear for months. Since she is a teenager, she has quickly outgrown many of her things from last year or even a few months ago. However, each time I held up an item that I called a "lost cause," my daughter would sound like a social worker protecting an orphan.

"But, Mom!" she'd say, "I can't get rid of that sweater. I love that sweater! You and Daddy gave that to me for Christmas two years ago."

Slowly but surely, I pressed on and helped convince her that it was okay to save some sentimental favorites but she needed to let go of the rest. Otherwise, where would she put the next sweater I might give her for Christmas or her birthday? She understood, and we made great progress.

Then she came to help me. You probably know where this story is headed, don't you, dear sister? Yes, indeed, when it was my turn I was not much better at letting go than my daughter Cora. She'd hold up a dress and say, "I haven't seen you wear this ever!" And sure enough, it would be something I'd worn five years ago but with which I couldn't bear to part. Slowly, my words came back to haunt me as I heard them from my daughter's mouth: "Where are you going to hang what you can wear if there's no room because of what you don't wear?" I learned my own lesson, and we removed all the items that no longer fit or that I no longer wore.

I tell this story to illustrate that so often we need similar help in cleaning out our "schedule closets." We pack so many things into our Daytimers, our PDAs, our desk calendars, and our memories that it's no wonder we set ourselves up for burnout. Frequently, I see more and more "life coaches" writing books and giving interviews on television. These folks always strike me as commonsense types who have a gift for helping others see their blind spots. They're good at cleaning out jam-packed closets and helping clients restore the pursuit of their passionate priorities. I'm not necessarily suggesting you hire a life coach (although if you can afford it, it may be helpful). But I believe your best girlfriend—the one who has no problem being honest and forthright with you—can do an even better job. Similarly, try consulting with your husband. If he knows you truly want his honest opinion about how you're spending your time, he should usually be willing to give it to you. (It's when we ask and then want him to reinforce the answers we want to hear that he seems reluctant to respond!)

And what do we do once we've cleaned out our "time closets" and reprioritized? It may seem like a silly question. However, many women get so addicted to the adrenaline rush of always running and juggling that they hit a wall once they stop. I believe we must focus on our priority passions and free up other time so we can maintain God's gift of the Sabbath for rest and worship. Let's consider what this means.

Sabbath Season

If you struggle with affirming and protecting your own need for rest, perhaps it will seem easier if you recognize how much God values it. From the beginning, our Creator gave the perfect example of what it means to set aside time for rest: "And on the seventh day God ended His work which He had done, and He rested on the seventh day from all His work which He had done. Then God blessed the seventh day and sanctified it, because in it He rested from all His work which God created and made" (Genesis 2:2–3). Our Sovereign God, all-powerful and almighty, Creator of heaven and earth and all that He placed in them, took a day of rest. He doesn't need rest the way our tired bodies do. He doesn't need refreshment as our weary spirits often do. He doesn't need renewal as our minds need time to process and relax from life's demands. But the Lord God established a day of rest and found it so good that He sanctified it. Setting aside a time for rest became a pattern and a mandate for His people later on after they were exiled from the Garden (I doubt He had to tell Adam and Eve to rest) and were wandering in the desert. It's at this time that Moses brought back God's testament for living, in which He declared, "Remember the Sabbath day, to keep it holy. Six days you shall labor and do all your work, but the seventh day is the Sabbath of the LORD your God. In it you shall do no work" (Exodus 20:8–10). For us today, it doesn't have to be the day we know as Sunday, but it should be a day or time we set aside for soul-tending rest.

Based on what I've observed in many women and experienced myself, many of us haven't often done a good job of resting on the sacred Sabbath. Often, Sunday is church day with all its attendant activities and ministry responsibilities. For some of us, it may be our busiest day—preparing lessons or crafts for Sunday school, doing sound checks and going over new worship music, laundering and ironing clothes for ourselves and our family, preparing Sunday lunch or food for a congregational celebration, getting everyone up and moving to leave on time. When my children were small, I used to sit down in the pew on Sunday morning and realize how exhausted I was from simply getting us all there on time! It's not that teaching, leading worship, ushering, and preparing food for after the service aren't wonderful, worshipful activities that can help you find balance. It's simply that they do not usually afford you the deep rest and time for reflection that is part of the holy renewal of a Sabbath.

Many women who have gone on for too long ignoring the command to rest, sidestepping the need of their bodies and souls for refreshment, may be called to an entire Season of Sabbath rest. Many pastors and college professors, along with some other professionals, often take such a sabbatical from their normal routines and responsibilities in order to recharge their spirits, to recover their passionate vision for their areas of specialty, and to restore the balance that has been sacrificed by overworking and overgiving to others.

Perhaps, while reading this, you're discovering tears in your eyes at the very thought of such a season of rest. But you're saying to yourself, *I can't just leave my job, my responsibilities at home, and my family and go off to a spa for several weeks.* True, most of us can't afford the time completely away or the expense of traveling to an exotic locale where we could be pampered and cared for. However, we can still choose to find ways to make our Sabbath season work. Similar to focusing only on passionate priorities, perhaps you can relinquish everything that's not essential in your life right now: no more committee work at your child's school, no more volunteering in your church's women's ministry, no more working overtime on weekends just to "catch up." But then you need to take the next step. Perhaps you could add in some things you've neglected for a long time that give you joy and peace: long walks, spending time outdoors, gardening, window-shopping, watching the sun rise, exercising, baking cookies with your kids, staring out the window with a cup of tea, building a snowman, going away for the weekend with your husband. If you simply set aside a month and took one item off your schedule each day, you might be surprised at how much time you'd have to pursue rest and balance in your life.

Soul Spa

Besides the physical and mental, the other component requiring true rest is the spiritual. Our souls need rest. Whether we're caught in a tornado of busyness and activity, or whether our emotions and spirits have been drained by a season of loss or disappointment, we need to allow ourselves to be still before our Creator and simply lean on Him. We need to find ways to revive our soul in order to maintain what matters most to us: our relationship with Him and our identity as His child. If we lose sight of these in the midst of the raging winds of life, it doesn't matter how long our tropical vacation is because we will have lost sight of our greatest pearl.

So how can we revitalize our spirits? I believe the key may be through discovering fresh ways to worship. Too often we come to associate worship with the many duties we carry out at our churches, or we compartmentalize it as something only for Sunday morning in the sanctuary. Perhaps we even feel guilty because we know we should pray, read Scripture, and worship in private, but again, there's simply no time. In order to recapture your passion for the Lord, I suggest that in certain seasons you take a break from your ministry commitments and simply allow your own soul to be fed. Perhaps you need to visit another church, or another of the services at your own church rather than the one in which you usually participate. Maybe some new worship music for your drive time would help you break out of the rut. You may need to spend time in the beauty of His creation, in a park or on a trail, simply praising Him for the multitude of colors, textures, sounds, and scents in the natural world.

As you allow yourself to worship and commune with your Abba Father, you will then learn to hear His voice again. Listening to His gentle words will enable you to restore balance in other areas as well. As you become more sensitive to the voice of the Lord, to His Spirit within you, you will also recognize the needs for each season of your life. When the Lord is your foremost passionate priority, He will help you know which calls to answer and which to politely decline. He will help you select the commitments and activities that are His best, not merely what seems good to you. In these activities, He will sustain you. He declares: "Come to Me, all you who labor and are heavy laden, and I will give you rest. Take My yoke upon you and learn from Me, for I am gentle and lowly in heart, and you will find rest for your souls. For My yoke is easy and My burden is light" (Matthew 11:28–30).

We can take great comfort from His assurance to us, dear lady. If we seek Him first, then we will have the rest for which our souls long. The work to which we are called is not to see how busy we can become or how many duties we can multitask at once. No, the real task of our lives is to stay centered on what matters most.

Mary Matters

Mary and Martha. Two sisters with different attitudes about what matters most. It's likely a familiar story, one that may even cause you a bit of shame because you know its message already in your mind but haven't allowed it to sink into your heart and your schedule. You may even long to be like Mary but find yourself compelled to be like Martha. Allowing yourself to choose as Mary did feels as though you're being lazy, inefficient, even irresponsible. At least Martha has something to show for her time, and, after all, she was doing it for the right reasons, wasn't she? I mean, if you knew our Lord was coming to dinner at your home, wouldn't you freak out a bit and want to do every single thing possible to make it a delicious, beautiful meal?

Why, then, was Mary's choice better than Martha's? Let's reconsider this story and examine why our Savior said the following about the two sisters' selections.

> Now it happened as they went that He entered a certain village; and a certain woman named Martha welcomed Him into her house. And she had a sister called Mary, who also sat at Jesus' feet and heard His word.
>
> But Martha was distracted with much serving, and she approached Him and said, "Lord, do You not care that my sister has left me to serve alone? Therefore tell her to help me."
>
> And Jesus answered and said to her, "Martha, Martha, you are worried and troubled about many things. But one thing is needed, and Mary has chosen that good part, which will not be taken away from her." (Luke 10:38–42)

So much to be done, girlfriend! And without any of the modern conveniences we take for granted. Martha had no microwave, no refrigerator, no prepared food from the grocery store, restaurant, or deli. No washing machine or dryer for table linens and kitchen towels. No, she was doing everything the old-fashioned way—by hand. Selecting and washing the olives and figs, cleaning and preparing the lamb, finding and mixing the herbs, sifting flour and kneading the dough for bread. Sweeping and dusting. Washing and cleaning. Juggling on her very own tightrope—just like all of us—and thinking of how nice it would be to have some help. Where was that sister of hers? What could Mary possibly be doing that would justify not helping her sister prepare for dinner with the Messiah?

We know the answer, my sister, but it still makes us a bit uncomfortable. Mary was sitting at the feet of the Messiah. She was worshiping and listening. She was obeying the higher call. She had no regrets because she was spending her time on something that would never be taken away from her. And despite how uncomfortable it may have been to watch her sister, Martha, sigh and flit back and forth throughout the house, Mary had selected the "good part" that would be treasured in her heart forever.

How often have we felt so all alone and envied those who seemed to have time to enjoy themselves while we slaved away? How often have we felt self-righteous for doing what needed to be done instead of what our hearts truly longed for? It may mean that the laundry doesn't get caught up and the dishes aren't put away, that the meal isn't perfect and every dust bunny hasn't been swept away. But oh, what we will receive when we choose what matters most! The comfort of resting in the wings of the Almighty. The peace that passes understanding. A taste of His living water. The joy that comes from knowing who we are and what we're about.

You know in your heart, my sister, that there will always be dishes to be washed, meals to be prepared, laundry to be folded, and e-mail to be answered. And those things must be attended to. However, they should not become more important than basking in the presence of your Lord.

Me-Time for He-Time

Are you beginning to realize how much me-time matters to the rest of your life? Can you see how taking good care of yourself enables you to love those most dear to you with patience and kindness? If you want to remain standing beside your man, you're going to have to know when to rest. Like a marathon runner covering miles of ground, you must allow yourself to pause for refreshment . . . so you can give cool drinks of water to your running mate as well. Because he himself may not even know he needs it unless he's pacing himself with you.

Just as we've discussed about women, many men do not do a good job of pursuing their own me-time. They work and work some more, then come home and check e-mail, pay the bills, watch TV, visit with the family, go to church, and then go back to work. They've lost their vision for how to be spontaneous, how to have fun, how to enjoy simply being with you and the children. While they wouldn't admit it, many men are waiting on "permission" to be off duty for a little while. They want to rest and relax with you but see you caught up in your own whirlwind juggling act and feel compelled to keep up.

When you can provide a quiet, calm center to your home, your man will realize what a sanctuary it is. He will long to be there and automatically become more and more conditioned to expect rest and renewal on the homefront. It is certainly not your responsibility alone to make the home restful and safe, but it's something of which you must not lose sight.

When you spend quality me-time, you will also change the focus of your expectations to your husband. If you find ways to prune your calendar to pursue passionate priorities, making time for Sabbath days and seasons, keeping worship as a fresh focus, you won't be looking to your spouse to provide you with what's missing—something only you and the Lord can pursue together. You won't be tempted to pressure him into knowing how to respond in ways that make you feel calm, secure, and relaxed. Instead, your spirit of gentleness and tranquillity will likely facilitate and encourage him in pursuing the same for himself. Your me-time can enable his he-time. This brings balance not just to each of you as individuals but to your life as a couple. It makes it easier to share the same goals and to grow together in the intimacy your souls crave with one another.

So I encourage you, dear lady, to realize the importance of me-time and soul rest not only for yourself, but also for the impact it has on your husband and your entire family. You are not a saint when you try to do everything for everybody. No, you are a saint when you focus on the rest needed for our Lord to produce His wonderful masterpiece in your life. Allow yourself some time to move toward restoring balance by gradually changing old habits, releasing less important obligations from your schedule, and rekindling your passion for God. I encourage and challenge you to make one decision right now as you conclude this chapter that will facilitate readjusting your watch to me-time. Perhaps the following prayer can be a starting point for this change.

———————————————— ∽ ————————————————

Dear Father, You know my heart so well. You know the many burdens that weigh on my soul, the many commitments that collect around my heart, and the many obligations that clutter my schedule. Please remind me, Lord, of what is truly important. Reconnect me to the passionate priorities of my life: my relationship with You, my relationship with my husband, my family, and the areas of expressing my purpose and gifting to which You call me. Protect me from the enemy, who would use guilt and shame to prevent my rest. May my me-time never be selfish but always aligned with Your perfect timing and provision. Allow me to drink of Your living water, to feast at Your table that fills my soul. Permit me to rest in the green pastures that You provide and to trust You as my Good Shepherd, leading and guiding me all the way. Still me now before Your throne, my God and King, and let me relax in Your embrace. Amen.

———————————————— ∽ ————————————————

Questions and Suggestions

1. When was the last time you did something for yourself that replenished your energy and gave you peace? When is the next time you have planned such an appointment?

2. How can a balanced time with adequate me-time contribute to the other areas of your life? Your marriage? Your children? Your work? Your church?

3. Make a list of your top five priorities for the present season of your life. Try to narrow them down to one sentence each. Please, if you don't have taking care of yourself written down, then add it to the list! Post the list in a special place where you will see each morning right after you awaken. After reading it each day, commit to honoring the individual priorities with the Lord's help for that day.

4. Whom do you relate to more, Mary or Martha? Why is it easier for most of us to get swallowed up in the details of each day rather than remember the most important thing: sitting at the Master's feet?

5. In your journal make a list of three things you used to enjoy doing but haven't had time to do in a while: cooking, singing in choir, ballroom dancing, needlepoint, playing dolls with your daughters, refinishing furniture. Choose one of these that you'd most enjoy doing and set aside time this week to pursue rekindling this former hobby.

12

Affairs of the Heart:
Relating to the Other Men in Our Lives

It happens far too often. An acquaintance from church will come to me and ask for prayer and counseling. "Oh, Serita. I don't know how I got to this place. I love my husband and children, but there's this man I work with, you see, and we've had to work closely on this big project, and, well, one thing has led to another. What happened? What can I do now?" Often, as she shares her heart with me, it's clear that she never intended to have an affair or to build an emotionally intimate relationship with this man outside her marriage. It's also clear that the relationship developed gradually over time; it was not a sudden burst of electric passion as their eyes met for the first time.

We're all susceptible, because, no matter how much we love our husbands or how much we make sure our needs are met by him and him alone, we still must face other men in the various roles of our lives. It may be a coworker, an acquaintance from your gym, a friend's spouse in your small church group, or a sympathetic neighbor. It often starts by sheer circumstance and then escalates as your encounters increase in frequency.

You're working together on a project that requires overtime or traveling together. You're sharing common interests as you work out together at the same time during weekdays. You're making small talk as you stand on the sidelines at soccer practice. Then suddenly you realize how much you're looking forward to seeing him again. The work project or occasion that drew you together in the first place is no longer solely the focus of your conversation. You're becoming personal with one another, sharing aspects of your personality usually reserved for family and close friends. You may even confide problems and disappointments, perhaps even in your marriage. *He sure is nice*, you think, not allowing yourself to recognize that he sure is nice-looking, too. *It's harmless*, you tell yourself.

And maybe it is—if you increase the hedge between the two of you right then. But too often it leads to your finding needs met that aren't being met by your spouse and then finding yourself entangled in an affair of the heart from which there are no easy exits. Whether it's full-blown adultery or an emotional affair of the heart, the effect is the same, and the sin is the same. For that reason you must focus on protecting your garden of the heart and keeping it safe and secure for the one to whom you're committed. Only your husband has the key to the gate of your relational garden.

This chapter would be unnecessary if we could manage to firmly grasp our true identity, focus on our marriages, and maintain balance in our lives. We would then naturally relate to the other men in our lives with confidence, compassion, and conviction. However, we know that's easier said than done. Too often when life starts to churn out of control, we find ourselves placed in situations with other men who hold the potential to meet needs that are being neglected in other areas. We know we have a problem when we're spending more time with our bosses than with our husbands. It should be a warning sign when we turn to our pastors more than our spouses to confide our secrets. We mustn't fool ourselves into ignoring the stirrings in our hearts for those male friends on the ministry committee, especially when we're going over the budget report at a candlelit dinner meeting.

However, I don't want you to think we should always view every man in our lives beside our husbands with suspicion and fear, as if they're predators waiting to steal us away or as if we ourselves can't be trusted. Instead, we must focus on the appropriate ways we can relate to these other men in our lives with gifts such as hospitality, modesty, and sisterly support. In order to give these gifts freely, we must also know how to protect our hearts from opportunities the enemy might use against us. We must determine our personal boundaries ahead of time and know how to maintain the sacred structure of our marriages. Let's look at several types of different relationships with the other men in our lives and see how we can set such necessary boundaries. In each type, let's consider how we can maintain healthy relationships with other men, protect ourselves from unhealthy attachments, and stand tall and unashamed as a godly woman before our Father the King.

Being the Boss

Serving men who are placed in authority over us in the workplace can present one of the greatest challenges to a woman's soul. It can also provide one of the greatest opportunities for us to ground ourselves in our true identities and to exercise our faithfulness to our husband and our integrity to our faith.

Scripture makes it clear that we are to honor and obey those who are placed in authority over us, even when they may not be leading in the way we prefer. In Scripture we are told, "Bondservants, obey in all things your masters according to the flesh, not with eye service, as men-pleasers, but in sincerity of heart, fearing God. And whatever you do, do it heartily, as to the Lord and not to men" (Colossians 3:22–23). If we view our boss as someone with whom the Lord has brought us in contact, then we can bring a gracious spirit to the work to which we're called. Hopefully, we can treat him with respect because he earns it, but if not, then at least because God ordains that respect.

There is a limit to such respect, however. If our boss misuses his authority to belittle us, to humiliate us, to harass us sexually, then we must not stand for it. Even though we may lose our job or be passed over for promotion, we will have our integrity and faith left intact. I know this is hard, dear lady, when the bills are piled up and your man has been laid off from his company, when the kids need new shoes and the pantry is bare. But you must take a big-picture view then. You must not withhold the truth from your spouse if your boss is acting less respectfully than he should. You must maintain firm boundaries and not allow them to be crossed the first time.

On the other hand, you must not look to your boss to provide strength or support that is lacking in your marriage. Do not be naive enough to believe your boss is greater than your husband just because your boss dresses well and wins the big deals in the boardroom. To the extent it is possible, I would encourage you to maintain a warm, professional relationship in the office that is distinct and separate from your personal life with your husband and family. This includes keeping personal or family problems to yourself, not confiding in your boss or other male (and sometimes female) coworkers about your troubles. And my advice is similar for segregating your work life from your home life. Leave the cares of the office at your desk and bring your full, true self home to greet your family and the most important man in your life. Discuss what troubles you experience in the office when it's appropriate or when your husband asks. Don't hide things from him, but don't make sharing your boss's personality quirks and business activities the main focus of your conversation at home.

Another dynamic may arise when the roles are reversed. More and more ladies are finding themselves in the role of boss these days. This is certainly wonderful progress as women's giftedness is recognized and placed in authority over others. Consequently, you may have to contend with how you relate to your male employees. I still encourage you to maintain firm boundaries between your work life and home life. I would also be careful about putting yourself in situations where you're alone with subordinates whom you admire and respect. You want to avoid all appearances of indiscretion or evil, especially ones that would fuel the office gossip mill. One young lady told me her coworkers gossiped so much about her time alone with a handsome coworker that the two of them felt isolated from the rest of the office. Soon they were confiding in each other and depending far too much on the other. Their emotional affair ironically stemmed from the very gossip that was unfounded when they were first relating.

Don't give anyone cause or opportunity to link you with another man. Unfortunately, an office can become a political microcosm where others will look for moments to exploit your weakness. Therefore use your strengths to shield your heart. Whether as the lowest person on the company ladder or the CEO at the top of the chain, I encourage you to remain above and beyond reproach. Don't compromise your femininity as a way of falsely protecting yourself or as a way of showing the men in your company that you're "just like them." You are *not* just like them, nor should you be. Don't be afraid to show your compassion and understanding, your ability to nurture a deal or envision a beautiful product. Don't be afraid to care about the people with whom you work. However, you also must not be afraid to be firm and fierce about what matters most to you. Don't hesitate to maintain strong boundaries and to exercise shrewd judgment about what needs doing. You are a lady, a daughter of the King of kings, and the wife of the special husband with whom the Lord has paired you. Keep this as your base of identity, and you will maintain the necessary balance to earn your boss's respect, your employees' trust, and your coworkers' admiration.

Attractions at the Altar

As disheartening as it may be, if we've been in the church long enough, we have likely witnessed a pastor or man in career ministry stumble with one of the women from his flock. Much of why it's so disappointing is that both parties obviously knew better and sought more for themselves in the Lord than what they settled for in each other. How could such a spiritual relationship as that of pastor and congregant, of shepherd and lamb, evolve into something so carnal and less than holy?

Perhaps you've never considered the dynamics of this relationship. All the more reason to think through it together right now. As we saw when we discussed the chapters on marriage and on lovemaking in marriage, sexuality is intimately intertwined with spirituality. When you are physically attracted and involved with a man, there is a spiritual bond that occurs to unite the two of you. Similarly, I believe that when a spiritual connection is shared, particularly in the intimacy of a counseling and prayer session, a physical attraction may be a natural response.

Consider this for a moment: Imagine how you would feel if you went to visit a man you look up to in your church—your pastor, perhaps, or someone on staff or even your Bible study leader. It could even be a Christian counselor. You visit with this man you already respect, and your appreciation for his wisdom, compassion, and godliness only grows as he listens to your heart. As you pour out your deepest secrets, share the most shameful parts of your past, and relay your most pressing fears, he engages with your story and hears beyond your words. A spiritual bond develops naturally between you as you view him as a spiritual father or brother in Christ. He respects your boundaries and treats you with nothing but the kindness of Jesus.

But then you start depending on him too much. You can't wait to see him at your next appointment. You can't imagine dealing with your life without his counsel and warm smile to reassure you. You tell him things you would never tell your spouse or closest girlfriend. These should be red flags to you, dear sister. Even if he ignores or rebuffs your unhealthy dependency on him, it can still turn out poorly. You may be tempted to entrap him or to spoil his reputation through flirtatious looks and sly comments in the presence of others.

Understand, he shares an equal responsibility to maintain the high road. He must not allow himself to be flattered and encouraged by your deep appreciation of the way God has gifted him. He must seek minimal involvement in order to make his contribution to your spiritual healing and well-being. That means he should include a lady in his counseling practice, preferably in the room with you during your meetings. This also means he doesn't meet with you alone, in private, where the enemy can try to tempt you both, temporarily hindering the good work God has planned. This means that he should limit physical touch or affection to public places in view of others, not in overly friendly ways behind closed doors.

Due to my husband's passion for helping broken women discover God's healing for their lives and their identities as His leading ladies, he comes into contact with many women. The vast majority of these dear sisters view him as their spiritual shepherd and respect his authority as God's man. They also appreciate his methods of ministering to them that are above and beyond reproach. Occasionally, however, it's clear that some women would seek to grow too close to him. This is where his judgment and my complete trust in him form a necessary protective boundary. If ladies insist on meeting with him alone, he views it as a red flag. And he can discern the difference between a hurting heart that needs privacy and discretion and one that seeks an intimacy both inappropriate and not of God.

Spiritual counsel and godly leadership can have a profound effect on your personal growth, your awareness of your true identity, your giftedness, and your marriage relationship. I don't want to discourage you in any way from seeking pastoral care. However, protect yourself by seeking counsel from other, often older, wise sisters in the faith. Include your husband when possible.

In your dealings with pastors and ministers, I encourage you to treat them as you would your own family members. Relate to them as spiritual brothers and godly fathers, not as boyfriends and sugar daddies. Be honest about what your heart is up to when you interact with them, and don't go looking for something you need to work on at home with your husband. You will grow in your faith and receive numerous blessings if you allow yourself to be part of the family of God's wonderful children.

Just Friends

Perhaps the most difficult category to address in how we relate to other men has to do with those gentlemen we consider as "just friends." These relationships spring from many sources. Some may come from our church, some from former jobs, some from our hometowns, some from college and high school. We may even have dated some of them before we married our husbands. How are we to regard these men in our lives and our involvement with them? Is it even possible to have a "platonic" friendship with other men, or should we avoid such relationships altogether?

First, let me say that I believe it's next to impossible to entirely avoid interacting with male friends. If we're so afraid of succumbing to an emotional affair, we need to squarely face those issues in our marriage. And I believe that if we rule out the category of friendship with other men, we are robbing ourselves of many blessings the Lord provides for us through such gifts. Through some of the male friends in my life, I have learned more about how men think and see the world, why my husband and sons behave the way they do, and how I am perceived by others. I have also enjoyed the benefits of laughter, insight into God's Word, and the blessing of hearing how the Lord is working in others' lives through my male friends.

Having commented on those rich benefits, however, let me once again balance it with some words of caution. One older church mother gave me words of wisdom that I've never forgotten on how to relate to men as brothers in Christ. She said, "Young lady, don't be afraid to have male friends beside your husband. However, don't forget that you'll never have another best friend besides your husband." Her words seemed simple and obvious at the time, but as I've grown in various seasons and friendships over the years, the wisdom of her words has grown in strength. Sometimes it seems to take more effort on my part to cultivate friendship with my husband, who knows my fears and weaknesses, my failings and shortcomings, better than anyone.

Caught up in the busyness of life, it becomes tempting to overlook your husband's friendship and take him for granted, to view him as a permanent houseguest, provider, and father of your children, and to lose sight of him as your best friend. In my conversation with this dear church mother, she shared about her relationship with her husband, who had recently passed away. With tears in her eyes, and mine, she related how seasons of life change, but friendship with one another becomes an anchor holding you together. "The romance and passion may ebb and flow, the children grow up and leave, the finances go up and down with the stock market, but your friendship is forever," she said to me.

I cherish that conversation and treasure its wisdom. So

please allow me to turn up the volume and repeat the message: Dear lady, you will never have another friend like your husband! Cherish and cultivate that friendship. Keep communication flowing and open. Practice patience and forgiveness. Become a good listener and an honest speaker. Share your hopes and dreams, your silly sides and your unself-conscious this-is-who-I-am self with him. Make a place for your friendship with your spouse to flourish, no matter what circumstances may bring. Place strong stone walls around this garden of your relationship and make two keys, one for each of you. No one else gets to come in and share the hard work of cultivating the beauty of your garden. No one else gets to relish the delicious fruit that only the two of you can harvest together with the Lord's blessings.

With your garden in place and carefully secured, your primary male friendship then becomes a standard without compare. Other male friends may enjoy your company, but you aren't building a garden with them.

My main point here is that we should enjoy other men as friends, but we must not have expectations on par with what we enjoy with our husband. And I encourage you to identify your boundaries and know when things are getting too close to the edge. Don't practice flirtatious conversation. Don't elevate a male friend's compliment on your appearance. Don't look to him to meet your most important needs. Be wary of men who seem strong in the areas of potential weakness in your husband; you may be setting yourself up for a natural attraction. Be modest and appropriate in your dress (more about this in a moment). Draw your identity from God and from your husband.

For myself, I find one helpful boundary is to imagine my

husband or children are present in the midst of my friend's conversation. Would I be embarrassed, ashamed, or uncomfortable if my husband were there in our midst? In one sense he is present, since he is part of the oneness we share. He's present in being my other half, my complement, just as the Lord is present as well. If there's anything that makes me the least bit uncomfortable, I try to listen to my heart and redirect the course of the conversation or interaction. In some cases, I have ended the friendship altogether if it became clear that the gentleman didn't wish to respect my boundaries. I try to talk openly about my male friends to my husband and keep nothing hidden—no inside jokes, no past history, nothing that could potentially drive a wedge between me and the man who matters most in my life.

Heart of Hospitality

Lest you think there are too many dangers in relating to the other men in our lives, consider how much we have to give to our relationships. As we consider appropriate and godly ways to relate to any men in our lives, whether they be from our office, our church, or our neighborhood, certainly one common denominator is hospitality. Please don't get me wrong and believe I'm simply being old-fashioned or even sexist. I realize hospitality is a special gift and that it comes more easily for some of us than others. I realize, too, that it is not just the gift of women. Nonetheless, I believe the elements contributing to hospitality—warmth, compassion, thoughtfulness, kindness, and generosity—can enhance our presence in the lives of other men. Let's explore these traits as demonstrated by one of the warmest receptions Jesus ever received.

> Then one of the Pharisees asked Him to eat with him. And He went to the Pharisee's house, and sat down to eat.
>
> And behold, a woman in the city who was a sinner, when she knew that Jesus sat at the table in the Pharisee's house, brought an alabaster flask of fragrant oil, and stood at His feet behind Him weeping; and she began to wash His feet with her tears, and wiped them with the hair of her head; and she kissed His feet and anointed them with the fragrant oil. (Luke 7:36–38)

This is certainly not the way most of us greet our guests at a dinner party, nor should it be. This is a broken woman expressing her love for her Master. However, I believe several of the traits she demonstrates are applicable to us as women with a spirit of hospitality. Most important, I believe it's significant that she recognized the occasion and came prepared. She knew Jesus was going to be at the Pharisee's house, and she brought her alabaster flask of most precious, perfumed oil. Without falling into the trap of perfectionism, I believe it's a sign of thoughtfulness when a hostess anticipates her guests' needs. She's empathetic and in touch with how weary a traveling visitor may be, how hungry a hardworking guest will be, how bored a child can get without attention. At the risk of being immodest, I'll confess that I entertain many visitors in my role as First Lady of The Potter's House and receive many compliments from these guests. And I attribute it all to the Lord's glory because I know that I'm not the greatest gourmet chef or incredible entertainer, but rather simply a good, down-home-style cook who tries to anticipate what my guests will enjoy. I'm not someone who can weave my own baskets, grow my own roses, and make every craft project in the magazines. But

I am a woman who appreciates beauty and enjoys creating a peaceful and inviting atmosphere for my family and friends.

What I'm trying to explain, my friend, is that we don't have to be specifically gifted in the culinary arts or interior design to show others respect and honor in how we relate. This shines through in the woman's response to Jesus. She served him. She came bearing her expensive gift, and she sacrificed her pride by giving of herself. One of the ways in which we are called to relate to the other men in our lives is through sacrificial service. I'm not saying we have to undertake a painstaking sacrifice for every coworker, boss, pastor, Bible study leader, and male friend. But our attitude can be one of generosity and kindness. Men appreciate this and are often touched by the gifts we choose to give them—gifts of gratitude for their presence, an anticipation of their needs, generosity of provision, and the sacrifice of our time, energy, and resources.

In fact, these are the gifts that Jesus Himself complimented the woman on when Simon the Pharisee grumbled about His interaction with her and the divine forgiveness He extended to her.

> Then He turned to the woman and said to Simon, "Do you see this woman? I entered your house; you gave Me no water for My feet, but she has washed My feet with her tears and wiped them with the hair of her head. You gave Me no kiss, but this woman has not ceased to kiss My feet since the time I came in. You did not anoint My head with oil, but this woman has anointed My feet with fragrant oil. Therefore I say to you, her sins, which are many, are forgiven, for she loved much. But to whom little is forgiven, the same loves little." (Luke 7:44–47).

In sharp contrast to the lack of showing hospitality by the host himself, the woman who crashed the party brought the most hospitality to the guest. And why did she do so, according to Jesus? Because she risked loving—a lot.

I'm concerned that as I've cautioned you to be appropriate and careful with your male relationships, you may have misunderstand and thought I was encouraging you to cloister yourself away. That is not the case. No, I encourage you to love boldly in your gifts of hospitality and service. Don't be afraid to exercise your giftedness and demonstrate your abilities. You don't have to play it safe and remove yourself from the kitchen, the dining room, or the meeting when serving the other men in your life. You simply cannot love them as you love your husband. You must learn how much of your heart you can give and share with others while its entirety is saved for your Lord and your lover.

Relationship Reminders

For many single ladies, relating to other men in their lives causes great stress or uncertainty about how to proceed. If you're in a season of singleness at present, you may be thinking, *But how do I relate to these other men in my life if I'm not married? Is it okay to pursue them as husband material?* I may be phrasing this bluntly, but I trust you know what I mean. My response, however, basically remains the same: Don't view your workplace or the church as a singles bar. Avoid an attitude of expectancy and neediness that searches the eyes of every man you meet for the possibility that he could be the one. As we discussed in an earlier chapter, seek first the Lord and trust His timing for bringing the right man into your life.

Get in touch with hearing His voice in your life and fulfilling your purpose rather than making your life conditional on finding a man and getting married.

Then, with confidence in who you are as God's precious daughter, hold your standards high and maintain dignity in your relationships. I would also encourage you to exercise caution and discretion if you do meet an attractive, available gentleman in your office or at church. I realize for single ladies, though, this is often where they come in contact with most men. So, to the extent possible, I advise not mixing work with your personal life and keeping any potential office romance to a minimum. Similarly, focus on ministry and the Lord's work while you're at church or Bible study and then go on dates afterward, planning your time together as something separate and special.

In addition I caution single ladies, since they're often advertising their availability through their appearance, to practice modesty. Like *hospitality*, *modesty* sounds like an old-fashioned word, one that brings up images of Victorian ladies in high-necked dresses and long petticoats or photos of our grandmothers in loose housedresses with no makeup or jewelry. However, I believe it's a word better understood as conveying respect for ourselves and those whom we encounter. It's also about dressing and looking appropriate for the various settings in which we find ourselves. Indeed, it's often as much an attitude of modesty as it is choosing specific articles of clothing and particular accessories.

We find this principle reinforced by Scripture, where Paul said:

> I desire therefore that the men pray everywhere, lifting up holy hands, without wrath and doubting; in like manner also, that the women adorn themselves in modest apparel,

with propriety and moderation, not with braided hair or
gold or pearls or costly clothing, but, which is proper for
women professing godliness, with good works. (1 Timothy
2:9–10)

Does this mean we can't wear the pearl necklace our
mother gave us? Or braid our hair or pay full price for a beautiful dress? As I've listened to my husband preach from this
passage, I have grown in understanding that in these verses
Paul is setting up a contrast for some of the early Christians,
particularly the women. In the early church culture, many believers had come from immoral backgrounds, including cults
and idol worship. Many of these false religions maintained or
condoned prostitutes in their temples. To entice men from
their wives and from reputable women, these temple prostitutes would wear provocative clothing, intricate jewelry that
often depicted the false god or goddess, and rich, intoxicating
perfume. So in Paul's admonition to women of the church, I
don't believe he meant to give a specific checklist of what
women can and cannot wear. Rather, he was providing an example to which his readers could relate.

As Paul explains here, modesty stems from being known by
our character—our good works of Christian love, charity, and
hospitality—not by our fancy designer clothes and expensive
necklaces. As you reflect on what this looks like applied to
your life, I can't tell you specifically how to dress. My advice,
though, is to present yourself before the Lord and ask for His
guidance in how you adorn yourself and how you want others
to perceive you. Do you want the men at work to know you're
a woman of integrity because of your character and leadership,
or do you want them to think you're a hoochie mama on the
prowl? I realize the issue is often complicated by modern fash-

ion trends that focus attention on our figures, our breasts, and our sex appeal. However, this is where you must use good judgment and consider what is appropriate. If you're going out on a date with your husband, by all means wear a daring dress and bask in his appreciation of your beauty. However, if you're going to the boardroom, look professional. You can do this and still look feminine. Seek a style that combines classic good looks with your unique taste and personality.

Brotherly Love

Whether married or single, divorced or widowed, young or old, in all your relationships with men, I encourage you to cultivate a respect borne of your confidence and compassion as a woman of God. Don't be afraid to relate to the many wonderful men God has brought and will bring into your life. Allow them to experience your giftedness, your faith, and your hospitality as you relate to one another. However, think through what it is you're looking for in your relationships with other men. Be honest with yourself, with your husband, and with God. Don't exploit brotherly love as a means of meeting needs that should be met elsewhere, whether they be physical or emotional. Keep it pure, and God will reveal Himself through these other friendships and encounters with men created in His image.

May the following prayer encourage us to love the men with whom God brings us into relationship as Jesus Himself.

Dear Lord, You sent Your only Son as a Man into this world. Just as He was bathed in hospitality by the woman at the Pharisee's home, I ask that You would allow me to minister to those men whom You place in my life. Remind me first of my identity in You. And please strengthen my relationship with the main man in my life. Protect me from the enemy's snares as I interact with my boss, my coworkers, my employees, my pastor, my friends, and my other brothers in Christ. Keep my attitude gracious and kind. I pray this through Your Son, in the power of the Holy Spirit. Amen.

Questions and Suggestions

1. Who are the other men in your life? Besides your spouse and other male relatives, who do you encounter on a daily or weekly basis? How would you describe your relationship with each one?

2. What's the most difficult part for you in relating to other men? In which relationships do you struggle most? Why?

3. Together with your husband, plan a casual dinner party and invite the male friends you both value most. Have them bring their spouses or dates and let them know how much you value the role they play in your lives. Create a lighthearted, festive atmosphere with good food and simple decorations. Prepare a card or small gift for each man in attendance.

4. Go through your wardrobe with a trusted friend or favorite girlfriend. Seek her honest opinion about the image you project with your usual style of clothing, accessories, perfume, etc. Make note of her response and consider if that is how you want to come across to others. If possible, invite a brother or other male you trust to offer his opinion, too.

5. Who is your best male friend other than your husband? What's the basis for your friendship with this man? How is your friendship with him different than your friendship with your husband?

PART 4

I Stand Beyond Him:
Seeing Yourself
Through New Eyes

Wholeness from Broken Places:
Learning to Stand Again

The morning begins like any other. A woman awakens expecting the day to be another routine-filled course from home to the kids' school to work and then back the same way. However, like a satellite blasted by a passing comet, her orbit is shaken with the shock of sudden loss. Law enforcement officers call her with unspeakable news: Her husband has been killed in an automobile accident. Suddenly, the world as she knows it has been shattered into thousands of sharp, pain-filled fragments. There's no way to know how to even begin picking up the pieces and restore her life to its former beauty.

For another lady, the devastating impact of the passing comet may be a call from the hospital telling her that her adult son has been shot in a drive-by. For yet another, the shattering blow may be coming home to find her husband in the arms of another woman, a friend she thought she could trust as much as her spouse. Another woman perhaps feels the impact directly upon herself as the test results come back bearing news that she has breast cancer and must face the long road of chemotherapy and radiation treatments. Yet another must begin the slow, arduous journey with a parent who suffers from Alzheimer's.

If you've lived long enough, my sister, I don't have to elaborate upon this list of life losses for you to relate. You know some of these as your very own, likely along with others I haven't mentioned. You've borne the unbearable, life-altering blows of what it means to love others and lose them. You've been forced to discover for yourself how excruciating it can be to fall flat on your face and struggle just to get on your knees and utter a feeble prayer. You long to rise from the fragments and stand with courage, holy strength, and a hope for something only our God can provide. But how is this possible when disappointment and grief pierce your heart repeatedly? How can you get on your feet and stand when there's so much to keep you down? How can you know when to trust your man to help you back onto your feet? And what do you do when you must get back to your feet on your own?

Soul Scars

Regardless of the kind of loss we suffer, a scar is left on our soul. However, I'm convinced that when we lose the special man in our lives it leaves a particularly deep wound. We become one with him in our marriage and then feel like less than half a person when we lose him. Before we look at other kinds of losses and ways to survive their impact, let's consider the terrible grief that comes from losing our man.

Whether it's the devastation of losing our husband to a heart attack and facing the unimaginable prospect of starting over, or whether it's our heart that's been attacked by his infidelity and request for a divorce, we must face the truth: Loving the men in our lives carries with it great capacity for pain. There is no easy formula for survival. Each woman's grief will vary in its intensity and duration. Knowing we cannot uncover easy answers, let us nonetheless explore ways we can return to our feet and see ourselves with new eyes and a new vision of what it means to be not only a survivor but a testimony to God's faithfulness and goodness.

We begin this process of examining our soul scars by acknowledging the fresh tides of pain that often set us adrift from the security we crave. So often in the midst of the deep wound of devastating loss, the powerlessness of knowing we've lost him, it feels as if life will never return to anything resembling normal, let alone to a season when joy could return. However, we must not lose sight of the very real hope our God offers us. We must not succumb to the lies of the enemy tempting us to despair as we pass through the valley of the shadow of death. Despite how overwhelming our grief and pain may feel, we must trust that we can embrace our feelings and somehow find the Lord's strength not by avoiding them but by embracing them. We must also realize that our experience of such pain and hardship may be unlike anyone else's. In other words, while it's good to relate to others and know they may have survived the same kind of loss, we must also realize our feelings and the timetable for our grief are uniquely our own. A recent example comes to mind.

I recall accompanying a dear friend to a support group for those newly widowed. She had lost her husband to cancer after a yearlong battle in and out of the hospital, including chemotherapy and radiation. Needless to say, she was devastated, despite knowing her man was with the Lord and she would join him someday in the future. It took great courage for her to come to the support group and meet other women who had lost their spouses. But despite her misgivings and feelings of aloneness, in her grief she found great liberation in hearing the other women's stories. One woman had lost her husband five years before and still cried fresh tears of sadness over his departure. Another woman had remarried after a year and now felt called to help other ladies find comfort through the dark road of grief. There were ladies from all over the spectrum of grief and loss, and none of them pressured any of the others in the least to change before it was time.

Finding others who understand something of what we're going through can provide incredible support and sanity during those seasons of loss and subsequent life transition. Coming together with other people and sharing something of what we're going through may be the last thing we want to do, but it's often an integral part of our healing. And we can trust that, because they understand, they won't push us.

Another sure way to nourish hope is to recall the triumphant ways God has redeemed the pain and loss of other women before us. Indeed, we can start at the beginning by considering the incredible journey our mother Eve endured over the course of her life.

Double Despair

One of the ways our pain often lingers and haunts us is through our mistakes. As a result of our part in our losses, or what we perceive as our part in them, we often compound the painful consequences. Eve's first great shock to the system, as you'll recall from our discussion in an earlier chapter, stemmed from her own sinful mistake. And what a costly one it was, with repercussions that continued to ripple throughout time into our present day. But return with me for a moment to reconsider the devastation and hopelessness Eve must have faced when she realized what she'd lost.

Imagine what it must have been like to know the beautiful splendor of dwelling in paradise with your mate. Gentle rains falling to water the thriving garden of wildflowers in a palette to rival any artist's colors. The pinkest blossoms, greenest leaves, and bluest skies imaginable. The scent of lavender and orchids perfuming the breeze with their sweet fragrance. Animals roaming about only to be gentled by your approach through the wooded glen. Birds twittering and singing overhead. Your husband walking alongside you throughout this paradise, and your God revealing His love with a tenderness and intimacy that makes your soul sing.

And only one rule. The Lord told Adam and Eve, "Of every tree of the garden you may freely eat; but of the tree of the knowledge of good and evil you shall not eat, for in the day that you eat of it you shall surely die" (Genesis 2:16–17). When you consider how many rules we have in life today, we almost can't imagine having only one. God told Eve and Adam not to eat of the fruit from one particular tree. "That's all, dear sister. Everything else here is yours to enjoy, but this you must leave alone." But oh, it looked so good, and what a curiosity that they weren't allowed to eat from it.

That's when the lies of the enemy become so attractive to us—when the slithering serpent comes along and tells us what we want to hear, a way to justify what we think we want: "Now the serpent was more cunning than any beast of the field which the LORD God had made. And he said to the woman, 'Has God indeed said, "You shall not eat of every tree of the garden"?'" (Genesis 3:1). Often we set ourselves up for tragedy by focusing on what we don't have instead of what we do. Most often this is a case of what I call the grass-is-always-greener blues. So often we don't realize what we have until it's gone from us or until it's in jeopardy. We become color-blind to the rainbow of blessings before us and look for something that's missing. From my own experience, I've found this to be the case with ladies from every walk of life. They share their hearts with me and reveal there's something missing. No matter how wonderful her husband is, she can't help desiring a younger man. No matter how much money she has, she thinks she needs more. No matter how beautiful she is, she thinks she needs cosmetic surgery to stay attractive. We must combat these not-enough blues by focusing on the many blessings the Lord has given us. We must identify the smooth talk of the enemy as the deceit it truly is. Otherwise, we lose sight of our present and look over the fence at what we think we must have, not realizing how it may cost us our future.

For that's how our mother Eve found herself gazing at the gorgeous fruit dangling from the forbidden tree. Ruby-red and at its peak of perfection, it beckoned her. Enter the enemy to entice her through her own curiosity. He whispered the words she longed to hear: "You will not surely die. For God knows that in the day you eat of it your eyes will be opened, and you will be like God, knowing good and evil" (Genesis 3:4–5). Eve acted, and our world has never been the same. Adam followed suit as she handed over the delicious fruit, and suddenly they recognized their nakedness and ran for cover in fig leaves and the first awareness of human shame.

Talk about not realizing how much you've lost until it's gone! This poor woman expected to gain a set of rosy, God-colored glasses by eating the apple and instead found herself looking through the very mortal, broken lenses of her own deception. She had been duped by the enemy playing off her own weaknesses.

Have you made mistakes, sister, that resulted in your own heartache? Did you show more passion for your job than for your husband even as you saw him drifting toward an attractive lady in his car pool? Did you fail to discipline your children the way you knew God wanted you to, and now you blame yourself for their incarceration or drug habit? We all make mistakes, and we must not allow the enemy to use them against us. We are forgiven, and our Father lifts us up and washes us off, just like a beloved daddy helping up a baby girl who skins her knees by falling on the sidewalk. We knew we were running too fast, doing something we shouldn't have done, and now we face the sorrowful consequences. But we must get up and move forward if we are to fulfill our calling as God's daughter, His precious child.

Don't Dream It's Over

A large part of what makes our lives so difficult is the ongoing nature of pain. Often it seems we've just endured one loss when another hits us by surprise. It's as if we're trying to clean up the debris from a tornado and an earthquake hits. How do we endure loss after loss and the accumulated burden of pain they may create in our lives? How do we hope to see the goodness of the Lord in the land of the living as the Psalmist mentions (Psalm 27:13)?

Once again, we can learn from the first woman, Eve, particularly in the end of her story. Like Eve, regardless of how much we may have directly contributed to our own lost garden, we certainly have an idea of what it means to face the consequences. Eve's suffering was compounded by the pain she would feel in childbirth. The groans and contractions of labor became necessary elements of what it means to give birth. And she experienced them shortly after leaving the beauty and security of God's Garden as she gave birth to two sons, Cain and Abel. Certainly, there must have been a season—as they were toddling around, then growing into boyhood, and finally young men—when Eve reconfigured her perception of her world and her place in it. Despite the weariness of toiling each day to survive, perhaps she came to enjoy life again, to appreciate what she had lost and therefore to accept what she had. She and her husband had made a new beginning and a new life with their children.

But then Eve faced a double loss almost as devastating as losing her home and her closeness to God back in the Garden. One of her babies killed the other. Jealous of his brother's favor with God in presenting an offering, Cain led his brother out into the fields and allowed his anger and bitterness to fuel the hatred raging in his soul. He murdered his brother, Abel, and then lied about it before God. Like his parents before him, he tried to ignore the consequences of his terrible mistake and pretend as if nothing has happened. "Am I my brother's keeper?" he asked (Genesis 4:9). The Lord cursed Cain and punished him with a life of aimless wandering to the ends of the earth, away from his home, away from his parents, away from God.

Perhaps you can identify with Eve's plight. Perhaps you went through the birth of a child when you were not much more than a child yourself. You gave up the baby for adoption so you could start over and go back to school. Now you're established and the mother of other children. Or perhaps you faced a divorce early in life—either your own or even that of your parents—and then started a new life, a new relationship, and a new hope. And then you face another devastating loss.

Just as Eve lost it all again. Not just one son to the scourge of death, but her only other child as well. One murdered, the other the murderer. One buried in the ground, and the other buried in her heart. Can you imagine?

I'm afraid that far too many of you can imagine, for you too have suffered a double loss. You've started your life over again after one loss only to face another. Perhaps it's a second marriage that failed no matter how hard you tried not to repeat the mistakes of the first. Perhaps you've been widowed once and have now lost a second spouse. It could be having lost an adult child to the seductive power of drugs only to watch your grandchild fall under the same spell.

From my experience of losing both my parents as well as my brother, I find that each loss serves to compound the prior losses and reopen grief long buried. Certainly this is some of what Eve must have experienced as well. But God was not finished with her. He had other plans just waiting to be fulfilled in light of the choices she and Adam had made, even in light of the choices her son had made. We're told, "And Adam knew his wife again, and she bore a son and named him Seth, 'For God has appointed another seed for me instead of Abel, whom Cain killed' " (Genesis 4:25).

As you may know, it's not just that Adam and Eve conceived another child, but that this son became the lineage bearer of Jesus the Messiah. Out of all the deep wells of loss and sorrow, God did not abandon His children. Out of the sin that Eve birthed by giving in to the temptation fostered by the serpent, out of the pain borne of watching her own offspring banished for killing her other son, Eve likely didn't count on birthing anything else in her sorrowful life. But God found a way to redeem the deep soul scars of her loss and use her as His instrument in a far greater plan. Without her seed, her willingness to become a mother one more time knowing that she might be facing more potential heartache, she would have missed an incredible blessing. We're called to the same faith, patience, and perseverance. We must leave room in our life for God to redeem our loss. No matter how many devastating losses we've endured, we must not give up hope. Nothing—no, nothing!— is impossible for our Lord, He who was raised from the dead, who raised Lazarus, who turned water into wine and weeping into dancing. You never know when our Sovereign King is about to turn your pain around.

Love's Last Laugh

You know why I love movies with happy endings? Because so often the characters have endured much hardship and been tempted to despair, but then love breaks through and good triumphs over evil. I love happy endings because they remind me of the way God can produce a miraculous turnaround in people's lives. It's that kind of turnaround we see in Sarah, Abraham's wife. After the incredible, adventuresome life she lived as the wife of this man, Sarah was unable to give her husband the one thing they both desired more than anything—a son. And yet, what seems impossible by human standards is never impossible with God. Consider what the Lord had in store for her despite her own and her husband's incredulous responses:

Then God said to Abraham, "As for Sarai your wife, you shall not call her name Sarai, but Sarah shall be her name. And I will bless her and also give you a son by her; then I will bless her, and she shall be a mother of nations; kings of peoples shall be from her."

Then Abraham fell on his face and laughed, and said in his heart, "Shall a child be born to a man who is one hundred years old? And shall Sarah, who is ninety years old, bear a child?" . . .

And the LORD visited Sarah as He had said, and the LORD did for Sarah as He had spoken. For Sarah conceived and bore Abraham a son in his old age, at the set time of which God had spoken to him. And Abraham called the name of his son who was born to him—whom Sarah bore to him—Isaac . . .

And Sarah said, "God has made me laugh, and all who hear will laugh with me." (Genesis 17:15–17; 21:1–3, 6)

You don't have to be in your golden years to know the kind of shock Sarah must have felt when she found herself with child. She was ninety years old! She had observed and lived long enough to know about realistic expectations—and to carry and birth a baby at the end of nine decades was not one of them. But what strikes me is something my husband once pointed out: Both Abraham and Sarah had enough faith to fulfill their part of the process. They were willing to sleep together and make love with each other in faith. Despite how crazy, even ludicrous it seemed that they might conceive a child at their ages, they were willing to do what they could do in order to see the Lord work in their lives. And He gave them Isaac, whose name means "laughter"—for God enjoys surprising and delighting His children.

Are you leaving room for the gift of God's grace in your own life? Or are you afraid it's too late? You must not give up on your Seth experience or the possibility of laughter in your life. Even if it feels foolish to rekindle the sparks of hope, you must leave room for God's goodness to be birthed from your tragedy. Love will have the last laugh if you allow God to work His power into your possibilities. Jesus said, "With men this is impossible, but with God all things are possible" (Matthew 19:26). If you're struggling in your ability to imagine how God can turn your life around and transform the bitter dregs of loss in your life into the fruit of His love, perhaps the following prayer can express this true longing of your heart.

———————————— ⌒ ————————————

Dear Keeper of my Soul, You know what I've been through and how I've gotten to this point in my life. It hurts so much, Lord. Please pick me up, brush me off, and allow me to stand again. Protect me from self-pity. Protect me from the enemy's lies and my own fears of despair. Remind me that You alone have sustained me and provided for my needs in the midst of this sorrowful season. Please help me to have hope in Your plans for my life. Show me a vision of what lies ahead, that I might glimpse Your purposes and taste joy once more. Let me leave room for laughter in my life, room for the Seth experience You have in store for me. Give me Your comfort and Your peace that passes understanding. And most of all, I ask for patience and perseverance along the way. Amen.

———————————— ⌒ ————————————

His Healing Hands

As you endure your loss and begin to experience the Lord's provision through it, you will often discover the way He uses other people. Depending on your circumstance, one of the most powerful ways He intervenes can be through using the love of the men in your life. Often we are tempted to shut them out and endure our pain in isolated silence. This is especially true when we feel no one else can understand our pain or what we're going through. This also makes us more susceptible to the lies of the enemy in tempting us to doubt God in the midst of our sorrow. However, we need to pay attention to the loving presence of other people in our lives and the way God uses them to embody His tender care for us. Please allow me to share one of the most painful periods of my life and how the Lord used my husband to bring me through it to be stronger and more reliant on Him than ever before.

Although it was a number of years ago, I'll never forget the shock and devastation of the automobile accident that almost took the lives of my husband, my mother, my twin boys, and myself. When an oncoming Jeep veered in front of us to attempt a hairpin turn, our car collapsed like a crushed can. I watched in horror as my husband hit the windshield and my mother attempted to cradle my babies in the backseat from the impact. Then came a stabbing pain so intensely white-hot I didn't even know its origin at first. And then, as my husband climbed out his side of the car, blood streaming down his face from a head wound, I realized I could not walk or move my leg. Looking down as we awaited paramedics, I could see my ankle bone protruding and my heel crushed and displaced from my foot.

"You'll never walk again!" was the doctor's dramatic pronouncement during the days and weeks that followed. Time and again, for months and months, these bitter words and their paralyzing implication haunted me. Slowly I began to venture from my bed, but I could place none of my weight on the crippled foot. Most of my friends and acquaintances from church had grown impatient with my slow progress. I felt very self-conscious with crutches, cast, and one dress shoe on my other foot.

One morning I awoke and felt so discouraged, so resigned to my affliction, I crawled out of bed and began going through my shoes in the bottom of my closet. I was prepared to throw away all the right shoes, which I feared I would never wear again. The ugly brace that held my broken bone in place was predicted to be with me for the rest of my life. I would never walk again in a normal way. I felt so afraid, so alone and weary. I knew others sometimes pointed and stared as I came down the aisle at church or the doctor's office on the few occasions I had ventured forth. But one of my deepest fears was that my husband would no longer find me attractive. That he would view me as weak and passive, a victim of circumstance without the stamina to recover.

That morning, sitting and scooting along on the bedroom floor in front of our closet, I let the tears pour down as I sorted shoes and stared down at my despised brace. I didn't hear the footsteps behind me, but suddenly I felt arms around me, lifting me up and holding me. My husband's heart beat with such comforting assurance of his presence. When he finally spoke, he said, "I don't care if you never walk again. I will never leave you. I'll push you in a wheelchair if necessary. You are my beautiful wife and I'm so grateful to God for you."

I cried all the harder and unleashed the torrent of terrifying fears and desperate doubts from the pit of my soul. He soothed me. And then, with encouraging words and gestures, got me to take a step toward him. And then another. And another. He began encouraging me each day to push myself just the right amount. He challenged me to ignore the taunts of the enemy and simply do the best I could. Day by day, I drew strength from the love of my husband and his manifestation of the love of God. Over time I began to walk from the bed to the chair to the bathroom and back. Then from one room to another. Finally, I was able to throw away the ugly brace and wear a pair—a glorious *pair*—of beautiful shoes that both looked alike, that belonged together. Just as God had placed me and my husband together as a pair in order to stride toward His goal for us.

There have certainly been other seasons of loss and grief that have sent me reeling, wondering if I would ever rise and return to my feet again. But the Lord has been faithful to sustain me. He reminds me that there is nothing that can separate us in this world, no matter what happens or how terrible it may seem: "For I am persuaded that neither death nor life, nor angels nor principalities nor powers, nor things present nor things to come, nor height nor depth, nor any other created thing, shall be able to separate us from the love of God which is in Christ Jesus our Lord" (Romans 8:38–39). Consider these words and allow them to soothe your weary and hurting soul like a cool balm. There is nothing that can separate you from God's love. He will never abandon you, no matter how excruciating your pain may be. He will not forsake you to your numbing grief, no matter how all-consuming it feels. Pray these words in faith if you are struggling with anger, bitterness, or sadness even as you read through this chapter. Claim the victory Jesus won and realize your Abba Father will heal you and set you back on your feet to continue your journey.

Our Father delights in helping His girls become the

women He created them to be. The same is true for you, dear sister, no matter where you may be this day. Don't give up, and don't despair. Receive the strength and love of others that He provides. Feel His loving presence, and thank Him for what you do have. Recall the past times He has lifted you from the pit of grief and fear. And get back on your feet and step forward, knowing with His help you will stand taller than ever before!

Dear Keeper of my Heart, I am broken in so many places. You alone know how many hurts I'm carrying and how much grief hides inside me. Whether it's the loss of my husband or other loved ones in my life, You know how I ache and grieve. You know the small details I miss about those people and the impact their absence has on my life. I pray, Lord, that You would strengthen and comfort me now as only You can. Pick me up and hold me in Your arms. Give me Your peace that passes all understanding. Bind up my broken places and heal me so I may continue on my journey, never doubting your presence or goodness. Give me patience and courage to wait on Your redemption in my life, my Seth experience, my moments of experiencing the power of Your love. Use my hurts to drive me into Your arms and to trust You even more. Amen.

Questions and Suggestions

1. What's the most recent loss or painful blow you've experienced? How have you been coping since it happened? What do you feel about it as you read through this chapter?

2. In what ways can you draw comfort from others who have experienced a similar loss? Why is it so difficult to share your pain with others who may have tasted the same loss?

3. Identify the largest area of pain or loss in your life at present. Spend some time writing in your journal describing the source of this pain, your response to it so far, and what you wish you could do to overcome it. Share your journal entry with someone you trust and ask them to pray for your healing and recovery.

4. Pay attention to those around you and try to see if there's someone you can comfort and encourage during her season of loss. Consider how you can support her during this season: prayer, gifts of food and service, listening and understanding, and connecting her with other resources for support (church, counseling, etc.).

5. In what ways can you relate to Eve's life in which she faces painful consequences because of her own mistake? How do you blame yourself for the losses you've endured or are enduring? What do you need to do to forgive yourself and move on with your life?

Lasting Legacy:
Mothering and Mentoring Others

The room glows from the flicker of candlelight in beautiful centerpieces on each banquet table. The scent of roses lingers in the air. Crisp, white linen offsets the dark tuxedos the gentlemen are wearing and the elegant gowns of the lovely ladies. Upon closer scrutiny, we see that many of the guests are young adults, still in their teens. Later in the evening, names of various young women are called, and they stroll before the enthusiastic support of their peers and family, presented to society as young ladies, no longer girls.

It sounds like high society, a debutante ball where the affluent and powerful have gathered to pass the baton to the next generation of women in their privileged circle. But there's something distinct about this particular coming-out party. These young ladies are not the daughters of wealthy and famous families but rather faith-filled survivors determined to make the most of the opportunities before them. Most of them come from inner-city housing projects. Many of them are raised by single mothers and have helped raise their younger siblings. They have seen others their age join gangs, peddle crack in the halls of their school, and sell their bodies to help pay the rent. Some of them may even have tried these things themselves.

But now they're catching hold of a vision for a life bigger and better than what they've known. Their imaginations are being stimulated by seeing the beauty of fine art in museums, by experiencing stirring performances of the ballet and opera, and by learning how to look and act like a lady. They have improved their study habits and raised their grades. They have gotten part-time jobs and internships with companies that can fuel their vision for promising careers.

On this, their special evening, in a gorgeous gown of their own choosing, these young ladies are being presented to the rest of society. While many of the issues and painful memories of their upbringing linger, they now have tasted how life can be if they keep their eyes on the prize. They see a future and a hope that dazzle them with possibility and with the goodness of the Lord's provision.

One of my greatest passions in ministry is to help these young ladies see themselves and experience their lives as more than what exists within the dismal confines of a two-room apartment in the throes of urban decay. Together with my husband's support, we have established this unique debutante program to challenge and inspire these girls with God's best for their lives. Certainly, the new dresses and trips to the performing arts help. But most of all, I want them to see themselves differently, to know what it means to be able to carry their head high and walk into a room with a deep sense of their special worth. For each special young lady, I want to nurture her integrity and the character of her inner woman as she begins her journey from girlish fears to grown-up hope. I want to be part of a chain reaction as I pass on the wisdom, hope, and joy that my Christian mothers and sisters passed on to me. I want these young ladies to know what it means to want to leave a legacy all their own.

Midlife Meditations

As we get older, most of us reach a point where we begin to question and reconsider all we've been about. For our men, the proverbial midlife crisis has often been characterized by attempts to regain youth through irresponsible antics, flashy sports cars, and abrupt career changes. They may tell us they no longer know who they really are or what their purpose is. In many cases, we become the anchor points for them, reminding them of their marriages, their children, their responsibilities, their gifts, and their life of faith.

If your man is going through a readjustment phase, I encourage you to stay grounded in what you have together that is good but also to realize the need for change. As I've commented before, what you need from each other changes as the seasons of life change. As you stand beside your man, don't be alarmed if his pace gets out of sync with your own. Simply do your best to stay connected, to remain close enough to communicate, even as you journey at slightly different speeds.

However, you also must not be afraid to express your needs to him as you undergo your own seasons of change. We ladies are not immune to the same questioning of purpose that characterizes the midlife crises of our spouses. We may not have the luxury of reinventing ourselves through a new career, new wardrobe, and new identity, but most of us go through a season of longing for something that's missing in our lives. Perhaps our husbands are immersed in their careers, working long hours and traveling frequently. Our kids are growing up before our eyes, becoming young men and women and going off to college, jobs, and new lives of their own. Our own careers no longer seem stimulating or exciting; we've reached a corporate plateau that seems to stretch on indefinitely. We may start to harbor regrets about missed opportunities: the promotion not taken, the job not applied for, the phone call not returned, the e-mail un-opened.

Consequently, we may question all we've been about. Or, as we saw in the last chapter, in the midst of a devastating loss, we may come undone and not know how to pick up the pieces and begin again. Or it may simply catch us by surprise. I recall a conversation with one woman about my age at a women's retreat. I had been speaking on what it means to leave a legacy by what we sow into the lives of others. During an afternoon break, a sister approached me and asked for a few moments of my time. She confided that she was in the midst of an incredible season of transition. Her husband had left her. She had one son in college, and the other had moved in with his father. Her mother had died six months earlier. And so in less than a year's time, her life had come undone, and she was reeling, unable to find herself. She asked me, "What should I focus on? How can I begin to know what my life is all about? How can I make any kind of difference?"

We prayed together. But while she seemed more at peace and thanked me for our conversation, I was more troubled than when we started. Her questions were good ones and pierced my heart in a way I had not experienced. My twin boys had just moved out recently to begin new jobs and lives as college students. My own mother had recently passed away and left me feeling orphaned and alone. And while my marriage was thankfully secure and solid, I still missed my husband during his times away and realized I resented that God often got more of him than I did.

Although this dear lady never intended to pass on her concerns to me, I began to ask myself some of the same questions with which she struggled. In the absence of my mother, I felt an awareness of my own mortality stronger than ever. What difference would I leave behind after I passed away? Mamma had left me so much in terms of her character, her love and support, her kindness and laughter. She had instilled in me the importance of persevering in faith, no matter what life may bring. Now that she was gone, how could I pass these traits on to my children? What would my legacy be? These questions burned inside me with a new urgency.

It was during this time that the idea for the debutante program was borne. I wanted to find some way to make a difference in the lives of young ladies who struggled to know their life's purpose, who were starved for beauty and the hope that God held more for them if they sought Him first. Together with a renewed vision of what I wanted to impart to my own children, I found that my purpose and identity were basically the same as before, only sharper and more clearly defined.

As I've talked to other women and researched how we endure transitions in life's seasons, I've found my experience is not unique. Often what we need is not so much a drastic change as a recentering and refocusing on what was originally important to us. So often the temptation during these seasons of transition is to focus on changing the props, the scenery, and the costumes on the stage of our lives. Like a makeover session at the department store beauty counter, we want someone else to tell us who we are and what we should do. We want something new and refreshing to empower us and renew our sense of what's most important. So we find ourselves trying to keep up with our husband or with girlfriends who are already immersed in the process of reinventing themselves. Or we search for a new pastor, new best friend, or the latest self-help guru to tell us who to be and how to become that person. We want someone to define our legacy.

But only we can do that for ourselves, and only in the presence of our faithful God. If we stay connected to Him, even as we question and struggle with our place in His production, He will reveal His plan for us. He will show us how to leave behind a meaning and purpose that are contagious—that make an impact on this earth for His kingdom. For many women, I believe that purpose relates to our ability to leave a legacy in our children and in others into whom we pour ourselves. Whether or not we are birth mothers to the children in our lives, I believe we can find fulfillment in nurturing and mentoring them in the faith. Just as a champion athlete can improve her training when she joins an elite team, let's return to some of our great mothers of the faith and consider their contribution.

Legacy with Legs

In an earlier chapter, we examined the story of Ruth and her mother-in-law, Naomi. Most of our discussion focused on Ruth and her faithfulness as she waited on God's provision and found it in her near kinsman, Boaz. But let's return for a moment and consider the role Naomi played in all this. I believe we may find her startlingly familiar.

> Now it came to pass, in the days when the judges ruled, that there was a famine in the land. And a certain man of Beth-

lehem, Judah, went to dwell in the country of Moab, he and his wife and his two sons . . .

Then Elimelech, Naomi's husband, died; and she was left, and her two sons . . .

Then both Mahlon and Chilion also died; so the woman survived her two sons and her husband. (Ruth 1:1, 3, 5)

It's a tragic passage into midlife for this woman of faith. First, a famine forced her to accompany her husband and family into a foreign land in order to survive. Then she lost her husband long before she likely anticipated being alone. But she had her sons, and as they grew and married local girls, she had a new extended family. And then came the shock of losing not one but both her sons, most likely within a short time of each other. Now what had her life come to? She was left alone in a foreign land. She was no longer a young woman, for she made it clear she was beyond child-bearing age when her daughters-in-law entreated her to let them accompany her back to Bethlehem. She thought she had nothing:

> Turn back, my daughters; why will you go with me? Are there still sons in my womb, that they may be your husbands? Turn back, my daughters, go—for I am too old to have a husband. If I should say I have hope, if I should have a husband tonight and should also bear sons, would you wait for them till they were grown? Would you restrain yourselves from having husbands? No, my daughters; for it grieves me very much for your sakes that the hand of the LORD has gone out against me! (Ruth 1:11–13)

It seems Naomi had fallen into a ditch along life's roadside and was consequently now reconsidering her entire journey. So often when life's losses become the main focus, it's difficult not to become very nearsighted. The loss of Naomi's husband and sons eclipsed her view of other possibilities. Being blindsided by such tragedy had planted a seed of bitterness in her. She felt abandoned by God and wondered what would become of her. She was tempted to believe she would have no legacy, only the remnants of a life of one bitter loss after another.

However, it's clear to us as readers of her life's story that God has not forgotten Naomi or turned His hand against her. For He gave her Ruth, a daughter-in-law who loved and supported her as well as or better than her own children could have. Ruth clearly loved this elder woman whose life had taken such a dismal turn toward desperation. Certainly, Ruth was not obligated to leave her own country and travel with Naomi, but she loved her so much and was so responsive to this new God of her husband's family she wouldn't permit Naomi to leave without her.

Once they arrived in Bethlehem, it's clear that Naomi's attitude only became worse. When old friends and acquaintances spotted the newcomers, they asked, "Is this Naomi?" to which the older woman responded, "Do not call me Naomi; call me Mara, for the Almighty has dealt very bitterly with me. I went out full, and the LORD has brought me home again empty" (vv. 20–21). In the midst of her midlife crisis, Naomi reinvented herself as an embittered, angry old woman who was forced to return to her hometown because there was nowhere else to turn. *Mara* means "bitter," and Naomi fully intended to change her identity to reflect her feelings.

Dear sister, when life's circumstances and devastating losses collapse upon us, we have to change and grow into the new place in which we find ourselves. If we don't—if we live in denial pretending nothing's happened or we don't feel the pain—we will never reach our full potential. At best, we will simply drift through the rest of our lives like a paper sailboat on a noon-day pond, going through the motions as we numb ourselves from the harsh reality. So many of us view the new place carved by life's losses as a small, dark prison cell of misery rather than as a dark winter tunnel that can lead us to a bright, open expanse of new spring life.

Have you found yourself accepting the shadows of midlife as a permanent condition rather than a temporary layover on your life's journey? Perhaps you're questioning what you have left to live for and what your legacy will be because you feel life has been so unfair. You worked hard at your marriage, only to see your husband die a painful death to the ravages of cancer. You sacrificed so your children could go to college, but now they've wasted your money on a lifestyle far removed from what you consider godly. You devoted tireless hours to your company, only to be laid off in a listless economy with no severance package. You gave your man second chances and worked to forgive him, only to be taken for a fool and betrayed again. You've reached middle age or see it looming up ahead, and you wonder where your dreams went, how they faded and dried up along the way.

But you mustn't give up, dear sister. You must not become a victim in a vacuum of disappointment, anger, and grief. You must pass through the hardship by doing what you can for yourself and those around you. Our legacy must have legs if it's going to withstand life's storms.

A Faith-Fueled Finish

We already know the happy ending to Naomi's story—the way Boaz admired Ruth's compassion and diligence and took her for his wife, the way Naomi lived to nurse her grandchild and to be honored and revered by her family and kinsmen. The same village women, those who had asked if this could really be the same Naomi they once knew, now bestowed blessing on her:

> Then the women said to Naomi, "Blessed be the LORD, who has not left you this day without a close relative; and may his name be famous in Israel! And may he be to you a restorer of life and a nourisher of your old age; for your daughter-in-law, who loves you, who is better to you than seven sons, has borne him."
>
> Then Naomi took the child and laid him on her bosom, and became a nurse to him.
>
> Also the neighbor women gave him a name, saying, "There is a son born to Naomi." And they called his name Obed. He is the father of Jesse, the father of David. (Ruth 4:14–17)

Consider this new season of Naomi's life that blossomed before her. It became clear to her that while her husband and sons were taken away, she was given Ruth, who gifted her with a place of honor and a seed to continue the legacy. Naomi was now esteemed by those around her, who could see the Lord had sustained and blessed her, despite the bleak days when the taste of bitterness never left her tongue. And note two other aspects of this story's ending that emphasize Naomi's legacy.

The first was her ability to serve as a wet nurse for the baby. Earlier, the older woman had commented that she was past the years of childbearing, beyond the time when she could give birth. However, her ability to provide nourishment and sustenance, both in the form of wisdom and counsel to Ruth and now in the life-giving liquid to this new baby, stood in sharp contrast. She didn't allow herself to become a postmenopausal shadow of her former self. She continued to give even in the midst of her bitterness. Such giving leads only to more life.

What are you giving your children and grandchildren? Are you still willing to nourish them on the milk of faith and the bread of life? So often ladies get to a certain age where they no longer feel useful. Their children are grown and live in distant cities. They've retired from their jobs. They attend church but don't get involved because they feel no one needs them. So untrue!

The other startling observation about the end of this story is that the neighbor women named the new baby Obed, meaning "servant," and declared him to be Naomi's son, not the son of Ruth and Boaz, although he clearly was. Out of Naomi's bitterness came service through perseverance and the mercy of the Lord.

If we backtrack for a moment to connect our starting point—Naomi's bitterness and victimlike attitude—with our ending point—Naomi's blessing through a child from Ruth and Obed—then we may be wondering what happened. How did Naomi manage to emerge from her midlife funk? While there is no specific answer to these questions, I believe Naomi revealed several clues through her actions in the heart of the story. Basically, it was a faith-fueled finish. First, it seems significant that for all her bad attitude, Naomi didn't try to stand in the way of others who wanted to help. When Ruth learned about Naomi's wealthy near kinsman Boaz, with his fields of grain, she asked permission of the older woman and received it. "Go, my daughter," Naomi replied to Ruth (2:2). Despite her negativity, Naomi allowed for the possibility of a better future. She didn't retreat and refuse to let her daughter-in-law pursue provisions.

Later, when Ruth returned with barley cakes to eat (left over from her lunch with Boaz) and grain to store and sell, Naomi wasted no time rejoicing in the goodness of the Lord. After learning the details of Ruth's day, Naomi declared, "Blessed be the one who took notice of you . . . Blessed be he of the LORD, who has not forsaken His kindness to the living and the dead!" (Ruth 2:19-20). How quickly she changed her mind, for in her heart, all along she had wanted to believe the Lord had not forsaken her and that He would provide for her according to His nature and providence. And she quickly got on board with what God seemed to be doing in the lives of her daughter-in-law and near kinsman.

> Then Naomi her mother-in-law said to her, "My daughter, shall I not seek security for you, that it may be well with you? Now Boaz, whose young women you were with, is he not our relative? In fact, he is winnowing barley tonight at the threshing floor. Therefore wash yourself and anoint yourself, put on your best garment and go down to the threshing floor; but do not make yourself known to the man until he has finished eating and drinking. Then it shall be when he lies down, that you shall notice the place where he lies; and you shall go in, uncover his feet, and lie down; and he will tell you what you should do." (Ruth 3:1–4)

Naomi quickly envisioned the possibility of happiness for her daughter-in-law, who had stood by her through so many trials. She encouraged the younger woman to make herself known to Boaz, to make herself as attractive as possible, and to present herself before him. As we discussed before, Naomi was not encouraging Ruth to be seductive but simply to be available. While she could have sat back and taken a passive approach, she offered advice and counsel that was clearly in Ruth's best interest. Naomi wanted to believe God was still working in both their lives, and she was therefore willing to risk being used by Him.

Later, when Ruth waited on Boaz to clear up the legal details necessary before he could marry her, Naomi encouraged her younger protégée to wait patiently: "Sit still, my daughter, until you know how the matter will turn out; for the man will not rest until he has concluded the matter this day" (Ruth 3:18). The same can be said of Naomi, ironically enough, for what she viewed as her life's tragedy had now become a story waiting for a happy ending. She was forced out of bitterness and into betterness, a place where God can use us to leave a lasting legacy for those we care about as well as His kingdom.

What will your impact be on the future, dear lady? Where are you in the midst of searching for your life's purpose in the middle of life? Have too many trials and disappointments left a bitter taste in your mouth? I encourage you to express the true emotions of your heart before your Abba Father, your Daddy, in order that you might catch a glimpse of how He is redeeming your life. You might find the following prayer helpful in this process of getting unstuck and moving through the present dim tunnel toward His future light.

———————————— ⌒ ————————————

Heavenly Father, I so long to leave a legacy on this earth. I want my husband and children to know how much I love them. I want my friends and spiritual family to know Your grace and goodness. But it's so hard some days, Lord, not to give in to bitterness and wonder if it's all for nothing. I know that's not true, but my heart becomes so discouraged. Please allow me to taste the grains of barley You've placed on my daily trail to guide me to the place of blessing, the place where I can

*nurse my offspring with tenderness and see my seed sown for the glory
of Your kingdom. Amen.*

———————————— ∽ ————————————

Losing and Lasting

I'll never forget one particular young lady at one of our debutante balls; I'll call her Rachel. Her story was not unlike many of
the other young women there. She had grown up in an alcoholic
home where her father often physically abused her mother.
When Rachel was ten years old, her father left and was later ar-
rested and convicted on drug charges. Her mother was faced
with raising three kids but had no job skills. Gradually, her
mother gave in to her own despair and then one day took
her own life. This young lady and her siblings moved in with
her grandmother—Nona, she called her—and tried to put her
life back together from the broken pieces of its beginning. Nona
was a lady of faith and suffered great anguish over the loss of her
daughter. And while she had never planned to take in a parcel of
kids and start over, there was nowhere else for them to turn. So
Nona provided a stable and secure home for Rachel and her siblings, and the young lady began to flourish. Despite the incredible loss they both shared, something beautiful had grown out
of necessity. A shy, nervous girl, Rachel discovered her passion
for reading and became an avid student, making straight A's
throughout middle school and into high school. Having taken
great comfort from the literary legacy of writers such as Maya
Angelou, Alice Walker, and Toni Morrison, she wanted to be an
author when she grew up.

On the night of the debutante ball, I watched as Rachel stood and thanked those people who had helped her achieve all she'd accomplished. She spent several moments fighting back tears as she described all the sacrifices, love, and wisdom that a certain woman had provided in her life. She went on to ask Nona to stand, and the two of them embraced as the rest of us wiped our eyes and whispered, "Glory to God." I can't begin to do justice to the amazing scene of one woman's legacy in action.

It reminded me of another mother who lost her child but then went on to minister to others. Our Lord's own mother, Mary, watched her baby boy grow from the infant in the manger to the Man on the cross. She suffered and wailed as He was nailed and hammered into place on beams of wood. She rejoiced and worshiped as He rose from the dead. And then she lost Him again as He ascended into heaven to be with His Father. But any lingering sadness could not keep Mary from giving the love and support she knew to be of God. It's always amazed me that in the book of Acts, as the Apostles gathered to receive the Holy Spirit, there was Mary, in their midst, just as eager as anyone to have her son back in her life, just as excited as John or Peter to share the joy that only knowing Him can bring:

> Then they returned to Jerusalem from the mount called Olivet, which is near Jerusalem, a Sabbath day's journey. And when they had entered, they went up into the upper room where they were staying: Peter, James, John, and Andrew; Philip and Thomas; Batholomew and Matthew; James the son of Alphaeus and Simon the Zealot; and Judas the son of James. These all continued with one accord in prayer and supplication, with the women and Mary the mother of Jesus, and with His brothers. (Acts 1:12–14)

What an amazing legacy! In many ways she had done her part already: She had birthed the Messiah and raised Him as her son. She was willing to be God's vessel and be overwhelmed by the Holy Spirit. She was willing to confront her fiancé and explain the miraculous, crazy event that was taking place in their lives. She had let Him go to become the Son of God that He is, had watched Him hang on the cross and then rise again. No one could fault Mary for not giving of herself her entire life. But she maintained the fervor and devotion not merely to finish, but to finish strong.

Can you see where you will be this time next year, dear lady? Do you know what your life will look like in five years or at the end of your days? I encourage you to consider the legacy you want to leave behind. Give prayerful consideration to what dreams the Lord wants to birth through you. When we mother and mentor others, we create an imperishable legacy that lives on long after we've gone to be with our Father.

Dear heavenly Father, I pray You would give me a vision of Your finish line, a glimpse of heaven that would sustain me as I run my race through the obstacles in my path. Give me stamina and energy to forge onward and to trust You to provide my needs and meet me in my weaknesses. Please allow me to model Your loving garments of praise and joy, even in the midst of the cold winters of fear and hardship. May I mentor others with compassion and tenderness, allowing them to see the cracks in my heart even as I testify to Your ongoing healing and loving presence in my life. I give it all to You, O Lord. Make me all that I can become and leave a legacy of faith for all who follow. Amen.

Questions and Suggestions

1. If you were to pass from this life today, what would be your legacy for those you love? Would this reflect what you want to leave for them? Why or why not?

2. Who are the women and men who have poured themselves into your life? What lessons have you learned about how to endure change from these mentors?

3. In your journal, explore all the ways you may have changed in the past year. Consider how these changes have manifested themselves in your life and how they have necessitated a change in how you live.

4. Volunteer at your church, a school, the library, or another program with young people. Offer to tutor, coach, or simply spend time with some young girls who need role models in their lives.

5. Why is it so much easier to change your appearance or image than to change or discover what's going on inside you?

6. In what ways can you grow beyond your life losses, like Mary and Naomi, and continue to pursue your passionate calling?

7. Make a list of your five most important life goals. Now work backward from the end of your life until today and consider what you're doing to pursue each one. Now track it as though you knew you were going to die in thirty years. In three years. In three months.

～ 15 ～

Final Stand:
Walking Tall Through It All

I invited some very special guests to one of my recent Woman to Woman conferences at The Potter's House. Other than my husband and the special ladies themselves, no one knew of my invitation. Since the conference began on Saturday morning, I made sure I arrived earlier than any of the other women attending. As the ladies began to enter, I watched as my special guests faced the stares and comments of the many other participants. Mostly they were ignored, except by the church security team members, who politely directed them to please enter the church or leave the premises. Otherwise, no one invited them in, offered a welcoming word, or inquired about their well-being. No one smiled. No one acknowledged who they were. Inside the sanctuary, none of the other ladies sat near them.

Perhaps you're realizing by this point that there was something quite extraordinary about my special guests. One was dressed in a loose halter top and miniskirt with tights and stiletto heels. Thick makeup hid her vulnerable eyes and bruised heart. Another was dressed in a threadbare housedress and dirty terrycloth robe. A regal hat with feathers and rain boots completed her ensemble from head to foot. Another guest dressed in men's jeans and wore a flannel shirt with hiking boots. She wore no makeup, and her short hair had just been freshly cropped.

Shortly after making announcements and opening in prayer, I shared the news that I had invited some special guests to join us. The congregation of ladies clapped politely and waited to see what well-dressed, perhaps famous, Christian leader, singer, or celebrity would join me on the platform. Reluctantly, my guests left their seats and shuffled down front. The gentle applause stopped, and I repeated that we needed to make my guests welcome. Slowly it began to dawn on some of the women in attendance that these were truly extraordinary women . . . whom they had overlooked.

My guests were gathered behind me in the pulpit by this time and, at my ongoing request, the applause continued as a sign of welcome and hospitality. More and more of the "normal" women in the church were beginning to recognize the women up front and tears began coursing down their cheeks. Slowly these "regular" women came down and began to embrace, to pray, and to lay hands on my guests.

An incredible anointing occurred and women began to cluster in groups right in the aisles and pews. Many of them joined the rest of us down front for prayer and repentance while others wept and cried out holy prayers of mercy, grace, and forgiveness. It far exceeded anything I could have hoped or planned for.

As the tears, prayers, and hugs gradually ceased, I invited everyone to be seated and began to introduce the special guests. They shared their names, and then I commented on who they appeared to be based solely on their appearances: a prostitute, a bag lady, a lesbian. I asked these ladies to forgive the rest of us for not welcoming them and making them feel part of our body of faith. Then I reminded us all that we were no better than these ladies. We were, in fact, just as needy and just as in-process as any one of my special guests. I went on to review the story of the good Samaritan—the generous traveler who was willing to stop and help another injured traveler (see Luke 10:29–37). In their self-righteous preoccupation with themselves, others had passed the victim by the wayside. The Samaritan, however, took the initiative to offer assistance and incredible life-giving provision to the wounded and weary man he found. He had tasted the love of God's goodness and mercy in his life and wanted to share it with those in need. I challenged those ladies at my conference that day to be more observant, more heart-sensitive to others around them. I also challenged them not to overlook themselves and their own heart needs.

I offer this challenge to you as well, dear sister. It's not that I want you to dwell on your past; no, just the opposite. However, neither should we rise above ourselves and pretend we're better than others and have no needs, fears, hopes, or dreams. As you may have guessed, my special guests at the conference were really actresses, but they represented an important part of us all. The parts that are shameful. The parts that are damaged and hurting. The hidden stories of where we've come from and the uncertainty of where we're going. The hope that burns inside us as a tiny faith-spark just waiting to catch the tinder of opportunity.

So much of being a good Samaritan to others has to do with

loving ourselves and knowing who we really are. We must be able to see ourselves in the places of others, in the wounded and hurt and discarded, even as we cling to the Savior's merciful provision in our lives. If we are to stand strong both as a woman created in God's own image and as a complement, a partner, to the special man in our lives, and as an encourager in our other male relationships, then we must know how to endure, how to avoid disappointment and to overcome self-righteousness. From my experience, the only way to achieve such an accomplishment is to be powered by the proper fuel.

Fuel for the Finish

In order to remain strong and walk beside the men in our lives, we must keep our eyes fixed on the finish line of faith. As I consider what final words to leave with you, I want you to recognize yourself as never before, to arrive at home with yourself. Most of all, I want to nurture the hope for a better life for you and a stronger, deeper relationship with your God and the men in your life. No matter where you may be coming from as you read these words, I want you to persevere in your faith and keep the hope alive. It's never too late for the God of the impossible! He delights in transforming our lives in ways we can barely imagine if we're willing to allow His presence to take control of our lives. This is why we must continue to stand strong and move one foot in front of the other as we live each day by faith. This is why Paul encourages us to finish the race that has been set before us and press on for the prize:

Therefore we also, since we are surrounded by so great a cloud of witnesses, let us lay aside every weight, and the sin which so easily ensnares us, and let us run with endurance the race that is set before us, looking unto Jesus, the author and finisher of our faith, who for the joy that was set before Him endured the cross, despising the shame, and has sat down at the right hand of the throne of God. (Hebrews 12:1–2)

These words remind us that we must expect and accept that hardships will come. As we consider our relationships with the most important men in our lives, we know we will struggle at times and stumble as we disappoint and hurt one another. Many ladies who come to me share that they are generally disappointed with the men in their lives: fathers who abandoned them, boyfriends who used them, husbands who abused them, sons who failed them. These ladies often sound ready to give up on men and ready to leave their faith behind on the shelf of their past. My heart grieves for these women, and I always try to remind them of some of the mothers of the faith we've discussed in these pages.

We recall our first mother, Eve, with her tragic failure and double loss of her babies, Cain and Abel. Surely she felt like giving up during those times. There were no other women to comfort her. She must have felt terribly alone and afraid, uncertain about seeing the Lord redeem her losses and restore her faith. But then came her Seth experience, and she realized a special gift—the lineage leading to the birth of Jesus, who has transformed the world.

Speaking of Him, there's His mother, Mary, a young woman privileged to birth the Messiah, God's own Son, but also anguished by watching Him suffer and die. Then to have

Him back, even for only a short while before losing Him again to His Father in heaven. But then she was there that Day of Pentecost to receive His indwelling once again, to have Him live within her forevermore. What an amazing roller coaster of emotions she must have endured.

There are Ruth and Naomi, a pair of ladies of the faith who endured incredible, devastating losses and lived to see their hope fulfilled through Boaz, their near kinsman. In Ruth, we see the power of love committed and channeled into God's purposes, the reward of risking and not giving in to despair. In Naomi, we see the ability of God to bring gratitude from bitterness, her transformation from the grieving Mara to the rejoicing grandmother of Obed, another forebear of Jesus Christ.

The same kind of endurance, risk, and reward emerges in the story of Sarah, promised by God that she would birth a son even as she watched her body slow down and cease its life-giving capacity. How cruel the promise must have seemed at times. And yet, God fulfilled His gift and gave her Isaac, His loving gift of laughter, in her old age.

Similarly, we see persevering faith rewarded in Esther, the young Jewish girl both lovely and beautiful, who was willing to save her people despite the consequences to herself.

Certainly, there are many more ladies, both in the pages of Scripture and in the pages of our history books and today's newspapers, who inspire us and remind us not to give up. With such a great cloud of witnesses before us, as Paul reminds us, I pray you will draw strength and courage to continue your stand and wait on the Lord. Ask Him to restore your marriage, seek Him for forgiveness for your father, beg Him to return your son to you. But do not give up hope—for yourself and for the men in your life.

Beside every good man stands a good woman. You are this good woman, so keep walking in faith and do not be discouraged by the momentary setbacks that may come your way. Remember God is faithful, even when we do not see Him operating in our lives the way we want to see Him. It's so tempting to be discouraged and to give up hope—for ourselves, our mate, the other men who have disappointed us in our lives. But we must leave room for God to work, knowing we won't always be able to see what He is doing. We must exercise faith and step out in the hope of who He calls us to be.

One of my favorite words of encouragement from Scripture comes from Paul's letter to the Philippians. It's a word I often love to share with the dear friends in my own life as they face hardship and need to be reminded there's more going on in their lives than they are able to see at present. Paul writes, "I thank my God upon every remembrance of you, always in every prayer of mine making request for you all with joy, for your fellowship in the gospel from the first day until now, being confident of this very thing, that He who has begun a good work in you will complete it until the day of Jesus Christ" (Philippians 1:3–6). Our Father does not give up on His children. He will continue to pursue you and to call you to more. He will continue to provide for you if you will seek Him in all your ways.

Dare to Compare

One way to remember He is changing you is to recall that you are not the same as when you started this book. And it's not the power of my words, dear sister, that informs my confidence in your transformation. No, my prayer is that the power of the truths I share here comes straight from His heart to mine and now to yours.

Dear sister, we began our journey together at the beginning of this book by looking at ourselves in our heart's mirror. Now I ask you to return to this looking glass once more, and be honest about what you see. Is your image the same as it was the last time you looked? Dare to compare where you were with where you are right now. Think back and assess what you see now compared to the image that gazed back at you at your last glimpse. What has changed in your countenance? Have any burdens been lifted? Do you see your relationships with the men in your life any differently? Do you see yourself more clearly now?

I pray you do. My hope in writing this book is that you would catch glimpses of yourself along the way. I trust you will consider the woman you've become by reflecting on your relationship with your parents. I encourage you to look for the connection between the ways you see your earthly father and the ways you view your Abba Father in heaven. Similarly, perhaps you have a greater awareness of the kinds of men to whom you're attracted and the pattern your relationships have tended to take in the past. Maybe you feel empowered to wait on the Lord and to stop living your life conditionally, frantically searching for the right man every time you look up. And if the Lord has blessed you with a man in your life, a partner and husband, then I encourage you to consider your current season and the inherent needs that come with it.

Finally, dear sister, I encourage you to be honest about the painful valleys in your life and the way you view those scars on your soul. I pray you have been able to replace the grief and bitterness with seeds of hope and joy. By no means do I believe you are now "fixed" and your relationships with men are per-fected. On the contrary, for many of you reading this, your heart has been awakened, and there are some painful issues that need confronting, with yourself and with your man. You may even feel more fearful about what the future holds as you look yourself in the eye and admit your insecurities and fears.

Wherever you may be on this journey of faith, I encourage you to stand tall. Cultivate the inner peace that comes from re-lying on the Lord in all that you do. Know your own worth in His sight. Nourish those dreams He has placed on your heart. Give Him thanks for the many provisions, of people and re-sources, in your life today. Gather strength for your journey and carry on, knowing you are a blessing to the men in your life, to your children, and to those around you. Your legacy will live on because of your willingness to pursue the Lord and His gifting of you, His precious daughter.

------------------------------ ✐ ------------------------------

Dear Soul Keeper, I've experienced so many feelings and thoughts as I've read through these pages and considered my own incredible jour-ney. I pray I would persevere to become all You've created me to be. Please unleash Your power within me so I might hold on to my call-ing and stand strong over the course of my life. Bless my relationships with men and allow me to be a reflection of You and an incredible blessing to each man, and woman, in my life. Please use what I've learned or been reminded of here to nourish me on my way and to keep my eyes on Your holy prize. Thank you, dear Father, for all You've done, all You're doing, and all You will do in my life. I love You and stand only by Your power. Amen.

------------------------------ ✐ ------------------------------

Questions and Suggestions

1. Review your expectations from when you started reading this book. How do you view yourself differently in light of what you've read and experienced? How do you view your male relationships differently? Why?

2. In what areas of your life would you most like to change? How have you experienced God's power in these areas so far?

3. In your journal, reflect on how you believe others perceive you based on your outward appearance. Try to imagine how your friends see you. As having it all together? As needy? Afraid? Confident? All of the above? Imagine how the men in your life would describe you, and why.

4. Spend a few moments prayerfully considering what has changed or been challenged in you since beginning to read this book. Write in your journal about these changes and your accompanying feelings. Share your thoughts with at least one close female friend and with at least one of the important men in your life. Consider who is in your life that might benefit from a copy of this book and send them one.

5. How have you changed since beginning this book? What perceptions or thoughts about yourself have been challenged or encouraged? What chapters and topics has God used to speak to you most clearly?